Preaching as Image, Story, and Idea

Edited by
Roger Alling and David J. Schlafer

With a Foreword by
A. Gary Shilling

MOREHOUSE PUBLISHING
HARRISBURG, PENNSYLVANIA

Copyright © 1998 by Roger Alling and David J. Schlafer

Morehouse Publishing
P.O. Box 1321
Harrisburg, PA 17105

Morehouse Publishing is a division of the Morehouse Group.

All rights reserved.
No part of this book may be reproduced
or transmitted in any form or by any means, electronic
or mechanical, including photocopying,
recording, or by any information storage and
retrieval system, without written
permission from the publisher.

Cover design by Rick Snizik

Library of Congress Cataloging-in-Publication Data

Preaching as image, story, and idea / edited by Roger Alling and David
J. Schlafer ; with a foreword by A. Gary Shilling.
    p. cm. — (Sermons that work ; 7)
  ISBN 0-8192-1750-6 (pbk.)
    1. Episcopal Church—Sermons. 2. Sermons, American. I. Alling,
Roger, 1933- . II. Schlafer, David J., 1944- . III. Series.
BX5937.A1P74   1998
252'0373—dc21   98-11344
                                                                                     CIP

Printed in the United States of America

Contents

Editors vii

Foreword (*A. Gary Shilling*) viii

Prologue
What Makes a Sermon "Really Work"? ix

Section I: *Discerning the Pattern, Making the Connections*

■ Attending to Literary Dynamics in Biblical Texts 4

"How Do You Read?": Preaching on Biblical Narratives
(*Thomas G. Long*) 4

You Will See Angels—Ascending and Descending (*Roger Alling*) .... 10 Jn 1:51

■ Honoring Moral Imperatives in the Spiritual Life 14

Preaching the Good: Homiletics from a Moral Theological Perspective
(*Thomas Breidenthal*) 14

Standing Out of the Way of the Gospel: The Martyrs of Lyons
(*Joe G. Burnett*) .... 20 I Peter 1:39
                                                                                   Mk 8:34-38

■ Celebrating the Treasures in a Faith Tradition 25

Preaching from the *Via Media*: Pursuing an Anglican Style of Address
(*Mitties McDonald DeChamplain*) 25

Comfort, Credibility, and Credentials (*Neil Alexander*) 32

■ Accessing the Energy in an Oral Art 35

Stick It in Your Ear! Preaching as an Oral-Aural Transaction
(*Neil Alexander*) 35

Tell It Again, Please; Tell It Again! (*Jane Sigloh*) 41

SECTION II: *Tuning the Senses, Shaping the Resonance*

- ■ PREACHING IN IMAGE FORM 50
- Going Home (*Michael Goldberg*) 50
- Your Presence Is Requested—Wedding Garment Required (*Penelope Duckworth*) 53
- God Is a Knitter (*Sara Scott Wingo*) 58
- A Certain Unmistakable Fragrance (*Charles Rice*) 61
- Martyr's Blood: The Martyrs of Uganda (*Linda Clader*) 65

- ■ PREACHING IN STORY FORM 69
- Be Not Afraid! (*Karen B. Johnson*) 69
- How Can This Be? (*Lisa Cressman*) 74
- A Bean Taco and a Cup of Coffee (*Sylvia Vasquez*) 78
- The Difficulty of Decreasing (*William Hethcock*) 82
- I Was a Son of Sceva (*James Adams*) 87

- ■ PREACHING IN IDEA FORM 90
- Flying Saucers, UFOs, and Alien Invasions (*Leander Harding*) 90
- Of Dogs and Divinity (*Stephen Weissman*) 94
- Life Is Difficult—Come and Live! (*John Conrad*) 99
- Tickle Me (*Richard McCandless*) 103
- The Messy Magic of Christian Community (*Joy Rogers*) 107

EPILOGUE: *Sermon Work as Sacred Gift*

- ■ THE STRUGGLE IS THE SERMON (*Ann Holmes Redding*) 116

CONFERENCE SCHEDULE 120

STAFF MEMBERS: 1997 PREACHING EXCELLENCE PROGRAM 121

WINNERS IN THE 1997 BEST SERMON COMPETITION 122

Editors

Roger Alling has been for many years a parish priest and a diocesan Stewardship Officer. He is President of the Episcopal Evangelism Foundation, and is Director of that Foundation's Preaching Excellence Program for Episcopal homiletics students. He has also directed the Best Sermon competition, another ministry of the foundation. For the first four years of that Competition, he oversaw the publication of winning sermons in the competition, and of staff sermons delivered at the Preaching Excellence Program, under the title *Sermons that Work*. For the last three years, with David Schlafer, he has edited the more fully developed preaching anthologies in that series. The two previous volumes are *Distinctives of Anglican Preaching* and *Preaching as the Art of Sacred Conversation*.

David Schlafer has taught preaching at Nashotah House, Seabury-Western, the School of Theology at the University of the South, and Virginia Theological Seminary. He has served as Interim Director of Studies at The College of Preachers. He regularly leads conferences for lay and ordained preachers, sermon listeners, and preaching instructors in a variety of institutional and denominational settings across the United States, in Canada, and in England. In addition to the shared editing with Roger Alling noted above, Dr. Schlafer has published reviews and articles on preaching in several popular and professional journals. He is the author of three books from Cowley Publications: *Surviving the Sermon: A Guide to Preaching for Those Who Have to Listen*; *Your Way with God's Word: Discovering Your Distinctive Preaching Voice*; and *What Makes This Day Different?: Preaching Grace on Special Occasions*.

FOREWORD

Many Episcopal laity and clergy believe that preaching in the Church needs improvement, but despair at the lack of attention given to this vital way of spreading the Gospel. Only three of the eleven Episcopal seminaries in the United States have full-time preaching professors.

For 10 years, the mission of the Episcopal Evangelism Foundation has been to help fill the gap. This book contains the fruits of some of our efforts. In 1997, as in the past six years, we invited the clergy in all of the Church's parishes to submit their best sermons. The entries were judged by the foundation's board of directors, and the top five winners, as well as their parishes, received cash prizes that were made possible by the generosity of the Honorable John C. Whitehead, former Deputy Secretary of State and an active Episcopalian. As in its six predecessors, this book contains those winning sermons, as well as the five runners-up.

I hope you enjoy reading these prize-winning sermons as well as the sermons and addresses delivered by the faculty and guests at our tenth Preaching Excellence Program, held in June in New York City. This year we expanded the program to include over fifty seminarians who show outstanding promise in preaching and who were selected by the deans and homiletics professors of the Episcopal seminaries. They spent an intensive week on the art and practice of preaching, led by six homiletics professors and six skilled parish preachers, in addition to well-known guest lecturers including the Reverend Dr. Thomas G. Long, the Frances Landey Patton Professor of Preaching and Worship at Princeton Theological Seminary.

This conference continued the ten-year pattern of high quality and great success, and Roger Alling and David J. Schlafer, the editors of this volume, have laid out the materials from this conference in such a way that readers will be able to get a sense and feel for the unique conference experience.

I believe that sermons in this book show that preaching in the Episcopal Church has gotten much better, but there is still room for more improvement. Please help us raise further the level of preaching in the Church with your suggestions and tax-deductible contributions.

Dr. A. Gary Shilling
Chairman, The Episcopal Evangelism Foundation, Inc.
500 Morris Ave., Springfield, N.J. 07081
(973) 467–0070

Prologue

What Makes a Sermon "Really Work"?

It's a good question, because many sermons don't seem to work. At least not very well. "Get a life!" we grumble, as one more flailing preaching effort struggles vainly to ascend beyond the edge of the pulpit from whence it is delivered. Then comes a twinge of sympathy or guilt. We have "been there, done that." We have preached lifeless sermons ourselves—and probably more than once.

Yes, of course, in the final analysis, the results of preaching are in the hands of God. And God promises (mercifully) to uphold human proclamations through the saving power of a word that "will not return void."

And yes, what "works" in preaching is differently defined and widely debated. No clear consensus on which sermons "work"—or why they work—is likely to emerge anytime soon.

The brute experiential fact remains, however, both for those who try to sit through sermons, and for those who try to deliver them: *Many sermons just don't work.* That is a source of frustration for all concerned.

There are surely lots of poor listeners out there; and a corresponding contingent of unskilled preachers as well. But moralizing about bad preachers and bad listeners doesn't really address the issue, does it? Most all the folks who face each other across a pulpit want preaching to work. And all of them, probably, within their lights, are doing the best they can.

It isn't helpful to moralize; nor is it all that efficacious simply to proffer a theological analysis concerning "the nature of preaching." One can write a weighty tome about what preaching is supposed to be, and still not be able to preach a sermon that works. Lining up a set of homiletical tools essential for sound sermon construction does not guarantee a preaching job well done, either. One can have tools ready to hand, and not be able to wield them very well. One can even have a competent grasp of the tools and techniques required for preaching, yet still not get the hang of how to work a sermon. A life of prayer is a pre-condition for the preaching life. So is a servant ministry that listens deeply to the full spectrum of cries from the heart constantly emanating from a preacher's faith community and cultural setting. Yet a preacher can be well practiced in making all these moves, and not be able to move the hearts and minds of women and men (to say nothing of stimulating the imaginations of children).

"What must I do in order to preach sermons that really work?" This is a common and anxious concern for some fifty Episcopal seminary students who come together each year in early June to undertake a weeklong adventure called "The Preaching Excellence Program." For over a decade, supported by the financial and programmatic efforts of The Episcopal Evangelism Foundation, these preachers-in-the-making have gathered, along with a dozen other, more homiletically seasoned colleagues. Working in concert, these preaching colleagues convene an intensive community of vocational discernment. It is a busy week. Sermons are preached and heard—literally—from morning until evening. Participants reflect almost nonstop on the theory and the practice of preaching—over meals, in formal presentations and informal discussions with distinguished visiting mentors, and in spontaneous energetic conversations with other seminarians and staff members. They seriously wrestle, and joyfully play, with critical matters of homiletical vocation. Everyone present experiences, in concentrated doses, the pulsing power of the preaching life.

No one leaves a week at the Preaching Excellence Program with a "twenty-five words or less" answer to the question, "What makes a sermon really work?" But they hear sermons that really do—and sometimes (to their own amazement) they even preach them. What participants usually take away from this conference is an almost visceral sense of how sermons can work, of when their own sermons are working; and of where they can best invest their energy in order to shape sermons that are well tuned to the music of the Gospel.

No conference experience can be captured in a book. As with any "high time" that takes shape in a live communal setting, "you had to have been there" to know what it was like. And yet it may be possible for us to overhear (and even to encounter) a homiletical "ah-ha!" that has direct bearing on our questions about sermons that work, an "ah-ha!" that connects with where we currently find ourselves—whether we are lay or clergy, preach regularly or occasionally, have limited or extensive preaching experience, participate primarily from the pulpit or from the pew.

Imagine, then—in order to establish a meeting point with the specific preaching community just described—imagine that we, the listeners to this book, are young preachers (young in preaching experience, but not necessarily in years). Imagine, too, that we are eager and deliberately impressionable; that we deeply desire to preach and to hear sermons that work, sermons where the cleansing, healing, empowering love of God is palpably present through the shape of the sermon.

It is now time for Evening Prayer on the first full working day of the "Preaching Excellence Program." We have already absorbed so much that our circuits are just about overloaded. Our appetites have been whetted, our imaginations stimulated, our energies stirred. Our homiletical anxiety levels, curiously, are both more eased and more heightened than they were two days ago. We strongly feel that we have never known more—and never known less—about preaching. We have never wanted more deeply to preach sermons that really work. And we have never worried more intensely whether we will ever be able to preach them. Who are we, unskilled as we are, that we should dare to hope we could really preach?

The Evening Office of psalms and readings, canticles and prayers, has been sung and said. There is a moment of silent space. The appointed preacher comes to the podium. She engages us with a gentle, wry smile, then softly but clearly breaks the silence:

Consider How You Have Fared—And Make the Move to Wonder

Anne K. Bartlett
Haggai 2:10–23; 2 Corinthians 1

> For the homiletically adventurous, the Daily Office Lectionary is just the ticket. Unlike the more familiar terrain of the Sunday propers, the Daily Lectionary beckons us into previously unpreached territory, texts less traveled. This evening is an excellent case in point.
>
> Consider Haggai, of whom one commentator tartly observed "a very minor prophet, indeed." A gentler critic wrote that Haggai at least "kept the faith in tedious times." That is no small task, we might agree.
>
> But then there is this: Haggai, it seems, knew much about modesty. But Haggai had a short-lived career which spanned only four (or maybe it was six) months in the second year of King Darius's reign. For a prophet, he was uncharacteristically taciturn. He only spoke out four (or maybe it was five) times, and two of those occurred on the very same day. A minor prophet, indeed,

with just one message to God's people: Rebuild the temple.

That's about it.

Haggai didn't fool around, he went straight to the top, to governor Zerubbabel and to Joshua, the presiding bishop that year. "Here's the word from the Lord," he told them. "Rebuild my temple. Oh, one more thing: I want it bigger and more beautiful than it was before."

Haggai ought to be the patron saint of contractors, the prophet quoted to kick off every parish building campaign. "You've been whining now for nearly twenty years ever since you got home from Babylon, complaining about how times are tough and crops are bad and good wine is hard to find. Well," says Haggai, as subtle as a two-by-four, "consider how you've fared."

In this strange scriptural backwater of the minor prophet Haggai (his entire prophetic output a modest two pages long), we find this thrice-repeated clue: "Consider how you have fared."

Prophets who are remembered, no matter how modest, how minor, how tedious their times, prophets who matter all say the same thing; they say: "Make the connections. Discern the pattern that is right before you. Consider how you have fared and then make the move to wonder where God is in your midst right now." And to no one is this message more urgently to be spoken than to a people beleaguered by their times, dispirited, deeply disappointed, and paralyzed by apathy.

Haggai speaks to those who are self-absorbed and in survival mode. We know something about all that. Perhaps times are tedious when we, like Haggai's folk, are caught like flies in amber, pining for the good old days, turning inward because we fear there simply is not enough to go around—not enough people in the pews, not enough money in the till, not enough leadership at the helm, not enough future to depend on, so we'd better hoard what we have and hunker down in our own little houses, as decentralized as possible.

Consider how you have fared. Make the connections. Dare to claim again your identity and truest selves as God's chosen ones, and come together. Leave the future to God, says Haggai. A new age is breaking in, the foundations are already shaking, the paradigm is shifting, and God's design will be imprinted upon us all. It's up to us to see it.

Now Haggai was wrong about the details. He was off on his timing and mistaken about the identity of the Anointed One; but what the heck, even major prophets got the details wrong a good deal of the time. Besides it's not the details that are crucial, it's the overall design. What counts is making the connections.

Prophets come in the oddest packages, are found in out-of-the-way places. I find today's prophets in the land of the new science, where the most astonishing connections are being made.

As a society, we may be bowling alone these days, self-absorbed, beleaguered, and hunkered down. But the new scientists are saying our attitudes and behavior are simply incongruent with the underlying design of how all life coheres. We're the odd ones out when we imagine we are individuals, alone and in disconnect. (Consider how you have fared, says old Haggai. Look for the bigger pattern. Rebuild the temple. Put God at the center, and do your part to make the pattern visible for all to see.)

Scientists now say—get this!—if two electrons, once connected, are separated one from the other, put in different fields, and the rotation of the spin of one of them is reversed, the other electron mysteriously reacts, responds, reverses the direction of its spin, too. This is a mystery, the scientists tell us. We don't know why this happens, they freely say.

Consider this: Scientists now say that if a butterfly unfolds its wings in Tokyo, the weather changes in Detroit. Scientists—the prophets of today, and they are not so minor!—our scientists now see that they were wrong all this time. Life is not made up of compartments that can be understood only when broken down into their tiny pieces; no, it's the other way around. All of life is so much of a piece, so much an interwoven web, that if one corner is but barely touched—or breathed upon—the energy vibrates throughout the patterned web, and all is changed.

Discern the pattern. Look for God in all of this.

One reason I love Saint Paul is precisely because he knew what Haggai claimed, that all was of a piece and needed to be discerned as such. Like Haggai, Paul knew what it was to be beleaguered, to experience life way out on the edge. When he wrote to those troublesome (and no doubt tedious) Corinthians, Paul first reminded them of their connections, one with another, and all of them in Christ. Haggai's temple for Paul transmuted into Christ's Body. The signet ring foreseen by Haggai—God's imprint on creation—that signet ring, Paul knew, was none other than Christ Jesus, who had been hard-pressed into the hard wood of the cross. When lifted up on Easter day, the divine design revealed itself, was made visible in our own time and space; so real we could touch him, feel the patterned nailprints in the body of the One to whom we belong; that same Holy One present to us now in the sacramental fractal of the bread and wine.

Don't you see, says Paul, don't you see that we are all in this together; and no matter what happens to any one of us, it happens to us all, because we are one Body. This is not metaphor; it is underlying reality. The connections are that real.

Consider how you have fared, writes Paul. Consider how this works: I suffer, I am consoled because I am held, embraced, connected to the heart of God through Jesus Christ my Lord; and that's what happens, that's how it works, that's the pattern. I suffer, I am consoled, which gives me grace to console others who suffer because I can give what I have received. The spin reverses over there because I am turned right here, and all is one. It makes no matter who is who, or what it is that happens, of sorrow or of joy, it's all the same design. The process and the pattern can be trusted with our whole being, because we are the Body.

(That's what I said, whispers Haggai. Rebuild the temple. See how all coheres, is held together in the very heart of God.)

In the temple, in the Body, all time is holographic, which is why worship is so central, because in worship all time collapses into

Prologue

the moment; and we sense in our own bodies, with this bread and with this wine, the body and the blood of the One in whom we live and move and have our being. The interwoven net vibrates with energy from faithful Haggai's time, passes straight clean through Saint Paul, comes to us as we discern once more the pattern of which we are graced to be a part.

It goes on today, of course, even in these strange, beleaguered times when we are tempted to crawl back into some old hiding place and bolt the door, and imagine we are all alone in this old world.

Last month a dear friend died at age 56, priest and rector of one fine parish for many, many years. As Bob lay dying, a parishioner spread out a quilt on the parish-hall floor and, with indelible markers, she traced around the hands of all who patiently stood in long lines for the privilege of being part of this loving pattern. Families put their hands one on top the other. Gnarled old hands of matriarchs and patriarchs were drawn, and tiny hands of sleeping babies, a pattern made of all the hands of the whole community of faith. And then the quilt was taken to Bob's bed and gently laid upon him; and as he died he received the laying on of hands of all the faithful ones to whom he was so incarnately connected in our Lord Christ.

Sufferings and consolations, it's all the same when we consider how we have fared, when we are blessed to see the pattern, when prayer provides the energy by which the pattern dances, the pattern embodied in this very world, right now, this day, this night.

Here's what I believe: I believe that our vocation—our holy task—is to spend our lives with eyes and hearts wide open, looking for the patterns, sensitive as tuning forks to the vibrations of the connections that underlie and overlie, and shimmer through and through this time, this space. As minor prophets—very minor, indeed!—that is how I think we preachers particularly are

xv

called; that is how we are to keep the faith in this tedious time, this extraordinary time, this chaotic time out of which the new life ever comes, rushing toward us over the horizon.

The sermon concludes; the preacher leaves the pulpit. The community remains in place for some moments of quiet reflection. Sounds from the center of the sermon continue to reverberate, generating a vigorous afterlife in the internal ears of her listening colleagues:

"Discern the pattern—make the connections! As minor prophets—very minor, indeed!—our holy task is to spend our lives with eyes and hearts wide open...sensitive as tuning forks to the vibrations..."

Maybe that is what makes sermons work! Perhaps our preaching vocation—whether in the pulpit or in pew—is to:

1. Discern the pattern of sacred presence
2. Make the connection with raw human reality
3. Tune our senses toward the mutual singing
4. Shape a sermon to resonate with the music

No. It can't be that simple. (Never mind that such "simplicity" is utterly beyond our reach). This is a sermon that really works! It sings in ways that resonate deeply with the prophetic melodies in Haggai and in Paul, in the stimulated imaginations of modern scientists, in the loving touches of suffering and consoling hands.

Yes, it does sound simple when this preacher does it. But good artists always make it look easy. We work very hard on our sermons; and they seldom work nearly so well.

Besides, "discern the pattern...make the connection...tune our senses...shape a resonating sermon": that's just artsy talk for what preachers always do (and usually with quite pedestrian results), namely:

1. Declare the timeless principle
2. Apply it to the sinful human situation
3. Find a "hook" that grabs attention
4. Serve up truths that are "interesting" and "relevant"

But then again, maybe it isn't exactly the same thing. Her sermon worked. It didn't just sit there like so many others; it skipped and danced. How, in our preaching, might we be able to do what she did? Not in her way with God's word, but in ours?

Perhaps the unfolding adventure of this week (and of this book) will speak to some of these pressing questions.

Section I: Discerning the Pattern, Making the Connections

Time out. Let's not get carried away. It is all very well to be swept along in the energy of a single, powerful preaching moment. But we will need more than a rush of warm feeling if we are going to discover how sermons can work.

To begin with, what's all this business about "resonance," and "music"? Preaching doesn't work with notes and melodies, with harmony and orchestration. Preaching deals with words and concepts, with sentences and propositional truth claims. The raw materials for homiletical artistry are elements like "biblical images," "human-interest stories," and "theological ideas." In order to preach, one has to exegete Biblical texts responsibly, to formulate a sermon thesis crisply, to amass relevant evidence comprehensively, to set forth arguments cogently, to illustrate points convincingly. There are, in fact, lots of ways for a sermon *not* to work; and a "musical" sermon certainly sounds like one of them! Come to think of it, we have actually heard rather more than our share of such "musical" sermons. We aren't just talking about those occasional Sunday worship services where the church choir performs Advent carols or an Easter cantata, thus giving the local preacher a welcome rest. We are talking here about actually delivered, seriously poor sermons. Shall we cite some cases in point?

- Sermons written in cute, rhyming poetry.
- Sermons that quote in full all five verses of a very long hymn.
- Sermons where the preacher tries to pass himself off as "one of Jesus' disciples...utterly enthralled by the Master's words on this lovely afternoon at the shore of Lake Galilee."
- Sermons where the preacher pours out a meandering, unending stream of free associations and archetypal images.
- Sermons where the preacher soothingly croons about how deeply she feels our struggle and pain.

In comparison with such musical mimicry, lecture sermons on esoteric points of theological history sound almost appealing!

In short, talk about "music" and "resonance" in sermons seems a messy mixing of metaphors at best. At worst, it sounds like a recipe for sentimentality—cotton-candy sweet, but insubstantial.

Sermons that work *take* work. Hard work. Conceptual, analytical, carefully reasoned work.

But then, so does the work of musical composers and performers. To talk about words and ideas that "sing" and "resonate" is not necessarily to utter an oxymoron. For instance:

- Think about a serious discussion in which we have been deeply engrossed. Then, out of the blue, one of us offers an astute analysis that "strikes a chord."
- Think of a story someone tells, a story that sets off strong reverberations in our own heartstrings, as it connects powerfully with the contours of a painful personal experience—an experience we had heretofore assumed to be totally unique, completely private, and damningly alienating.
- Think about a vivid word picture deployed in the lines of a deceptively simple poem, an image that suddenly orchestrates all the cacophonous elements in a tough situation we are facing, giving coherent focus to all the chaos.

Think about all of these. Now, can we really convince ourselves that words don't make music; that music, resonance, and preaching cannot be meaningfully, mutually informing? The question, obviously, is not whether sermons that work can be musical. The only question is how?

That "how" is what all the homiletics lectures, and all the sermons at Daily Office and Eucharist during the Preaching Excellence Conference presented in this book are about. Neither individually nor together are they the last word, the definitive word, or the whole word on how sermons work. But these homiletical words, these sermon words arise out of the lived experiences of scholars and pastors who really do work on their preaching, and whose preaching really works—at least a good bit of the time.

In this section of the book, we will encounter the engaging interplay of theory and practice concerning four important aspects of preaching. The four formal lectures and the four liturgical sermons re-presented in this section were all initially given during the 1997 Preaching Excellence Program. None, however, was paired with the other in that setting. (That is, they were not offered as explanations or illustrations of each other.) Nor were they, at that time, lined up under the headings which the editors of this volume have crafted and assigned to them.

In the continuing afterlife of the conference, however, it has seemed that, both individually and in relation to their designated partners, these lectures and sermons say a great deal about how sermons can work to "discern the pattern of sacred presence" and to "make the connections with raw human reality."

To pick up a question left dangling in the prologue: How is this "pattern discerning" and "connection making" any different from simply "declaring a timeless principle," and "applying it to the sinful human situation"? The difference is suggested by the titles of the four sections that follow. Preaching that discerns sacred patterns, and that makes vital human connections, does so because it:

1. Attends to literary dynamics in biblical texts
2. Honors moral imperatives in the spiritual life
3. Celebrates the treasures in a faith tradition
4. Accesses the power in an oral art

The interplay between the explanation and the embodiment of these four critical preaching elements will be allowed to unfold without editorial comment. If these lectures, these sermons, and the creative sparks that snap between them were in need of further elucidation, they would not work nearly as well as they already do.

PREACHING AS IMAGE, STORY, AND IDEA

ATTENDING TO LITERARY DYNAMICS IN BIBLICAL TEXTS

"How Do You Read?": Preaching on Biblical Narratives

Thomas G. Long

"How do you read?" Jesus once challenged a contentious lawyer,[1] and, we must admit, this is an interesting and complex question. How do you read? Is Jesus asking about pragmatics, the mechanics of reading? Or is Jesus perhaps exploring the lawyer's hermeneutical stance? Does the lawyer look for meaning behind texts, in texts, or in front of texts? Or maybe Jesus is pressing home a moral matter, the ethics of reading. Does the lawyer read selfishly or generously, with a mind open to the truth or merely scanning for opinions already in place? "How do you read?" Jesus wants to know; and, as the lawyer discovered, it is not an easy question to answer.

"How do you read?" is a challenging question not only for lawyers, of course, but also for preachers. Every week, preachers must read ancient texts and then stand up in front of congregations to say something that presumably results from those readings. To exegete a text skillfully is finally to read it well, to exercise suitable modes of discernment, effective strategies for allowing the stylus of the imagination to track the grooves of texts. Each method of exegesis—historical, theological, sociological, literary—carries its own set of tactics for readings.

Jesus' interrogation of the lawyer was initially about legal texts—How do you read the law?—but the real appraisal of the lawyer's reading skill came in narrative form. Jesus told the lawyer a story, the Parable of the Good Samaritan, and it was this story that turned the tester into the one being tested, that put the lawyer and his ability to read on trial.

Preachers are often in the position of this lawyer. We are given a story to read, a biblical narrative in which we are asked to find meaning. What I propose to do in this brief essay, therefore, is to think quite practically about a few of the ways by which preachers can go about the process of "reading" biblical narratives. Actually, I want to suggest not so much a method for reading but a beginning set of working categories, lenses through which the richness of biblical narratives may be seen. To be sure, categories alone are insufficient; labels do not make us wise. However, good categories do enlarge our imagination. They invite us to view narrative texts from a variety of vantage points, thus expanding the view and unsettling any single-minded understanding.

Years ago, homiletician H. E. Luccock described what he called the "jewel sermon," a sermon that takes a truth and turns its facets in the light; allowing first this, then that aspect of the truth to be seen. This "jewel" metaphor can be applied to narrative biblical texts as well. How can we take the jewel of a biblical narrative and turn it in the light so that its various facets can be glimpsed, revealing variety, depth, and extravagance of meaning?

From "Fortune Cookies" to Narrative Environments

Sometimes preachers make the mistake of thinking that the narrative form of biblical stories is accidental. It matters little whether the text is a story or a psalm, a proverb or an epistle, the task is the same: Reach inside and grab the main idea. Thus, biblical narratives become homiletical fortune cookies, pastry wrapped around one-liners. But, as is now widely recognized, the literary forms of biblical texts contribute to and participate in their meanings, and one cannot filter out the literary dynamics and forms of biblical texts without losing much of their power to impact readers and hearers. When approaching a biblical narrative, then, instead of fishing around in the text for an idea, the preacher should treat the text as a narrative environment, a literary space in which the imagination can move and explore, experiencing the impact of the story in many ways.

An essential part of this exploration involves such traditional narrative categories as plot, character, point of view, and setting.[2] In addition, however, to these broad, standard categories, there are other, smaller narrative features that can be illuminating to the biblical preacher. What follows is a discussion of four of these features, representative artistic strategies found in biblical narratives.[3] There are, of course, hundreds of such poetic devices, but these four can serve as examples to guide the preacher's eye:

1. *Repeated plot patterns.* Sometimes biblical narrators structure their narratives to guide readers through a developmental process of discovery. The preacher should ask, "What is happening to me as a reader as I move sequentially through the sequence of events in this narrative?"

For example, the author of the Gospel of John employs a repeated plot pattern that can playfully be described as "Question–Answer–Dumb Response." In this pattern, some character will ask Jesus a question (or imply one). The question will be a good one, but it will operate at the routine, everyday, mundane level of life. Jesus will answer the question, but he will do so at a different and higher level: Johannine Logos christology. Since the answer is pitched above the level of the question, it sails over the head of the questioner, evoking a banal, insipid response, thus, question–answer–dumb response.

A splendid example of this plot pattern can be found in a portion of the conversation between Jesus and the Samaritan woman (John 4:7–11):

Question: "How is it that you, a Jew, ask a drink of me, a woman of Samaria?"

Answer: "If you knew the gift of God and who it is that is saying to you, 'Give me a drink,' you would have asked him and he would have given you living water."

Dumb Response: "Sir, you have no bucket..."

To interpret this exchange only historically is to miss its power (and to do an injustice to the woman's intelligence!). The performative effect of the text is to cause the reader to wince (or chuckle) over the woman's banal reply and thereby to discern that Jesus does not mean the water in that well, the water that can be gotten by a bucket. He means another kind of life-giving water. When that discovery takes place, the belief-forming power of John's Gospel is at work.

2. *Repeated terminology.* The preacher should watch for words or phrases in a story that are characteristic of the author, since a word or phrase that appears in one story and is repeated two or more times within a document may gather cumulative force. For example, when Luke tells the story of the crucifixion, he reports that, at the moment of Jesus' death, "all his acquaintances, including the women who had followed him from Galilee, stood at a distance, watching these things" (Luke 23:49). The phrase "stood at a distance" (Greek=*makran*) appears at first glance to be merely a description of spatial distance; but this is not the first time that the Lukan reader has encountered this word. The Prodigal Son was "at a distance" when his father saw him with compassion (15:20), and the parabolic publican who prayed "God be merciful to me a sinner" did so while standing "at a distance" (Luke 18:13). In sum, the phrase to "stand at a distance" gathers narrative cumulative force, and is not simply a spatial measure but a theological

one, signifying humility before the mercy of God. This is underscored by Peter's Pentecost sermon in Acts, which ends, "This promise is for you, for your children, and for all who stand at a distance..." (2:39).

Another example of repeated terminology can be found in Mark 1:35, where Jesus is described as praying in a "deserted place" or a "lonely place." Left in isolation, this term could convey a gentle, pastoral setting, leading one to preach about the virtues of spending "quiet time" in solitude with God. However, the term used actually means "desert" or "wilderness," and, as if to underscore this, the author of Mark has already employed the term several times before its appearance in 1:35 (see 1:3, 4, 12, 13). In short, the repetition of the term makes it plain that this "lonely place" is no flower garden to which Jesus has retired for quiet devotions but is, rather, the feared Old Testament wilderness, the desert, where holy vocation is tested.

3. *Disruptive terminology.* More explosive than simple repeated terminology is the narrational technique of using words, phrases, or plot twists that are intentionally disruptive to the reading process. Narrators of stories and their readers (or hearers) have a tacit but binding agreement about how stories shall unfold, but narrators sometimes break this agreement for effect (readers can and do break the rules, too, producing idiosyncratic readings). For example, a narrator may intentionally plant ambiguity into a description, forcing the reader to struggle toward a decision about meaning, or may use a word in an unconventional way, forcing the reader toward metaphor.

Yet another way to disrupt the reading process is to plant a verbal surprise, an unexpected element, in the story—something like a linguistic "speed bump" designed to upset the smooth flow of reading and to jar the reader to attention. Just such a "speed bump" can be found in Mark 6:39: "Then Jesus ordered them to get all the people to sit down in groups on the green grass." Since the reader has been informed three times that this event is occurring in a desert (6:31, 32, 35) and Mark is not a "technicolor" narrator, the word "green" comes as a surprise, disrupting the reading process. Green grass in the desert?—technically possible but unlikely, an ambush of the imagination.

The first Markan readers were far more competent in the Old Testament than most modern readers, and Mark's little green surprise should be viewed within the range of their skills, not ours. When the desert suddenly sprouted green before their very eyes, two memories would ring in their ears. First, they would recall the messianic promise that the "desert shall blossom" (see, for example, Isaiah 35:1).

Second, the phrase "he made them sit down on the green grass" would reverberate with the phrase "he makes me to lie down in green pastures" from Psalm 23. That psalm begins, of course, "The Lord is my shepherd...," which connects the reader to Mark 6:34: "He had compassion on them because they were like sheep without a shepherd." The single, unexpected word "green" disrupts the normal reading process and causes two major Old Testament images to merge with the story and to illumine the meaning of Jesus' feeding of the multitude.

4. *Intertextuality.* Narrative intertextuality refers to the practice of making allusions in one story to another story, such that the two stories become mutually interpreting. For example, when Luke tells us, in the Zacchaeus story, that Jesus "entered Jericho and was passing through...," the reader is reminded of another Jesus ("Joshua") and another passing through Jericho.

Sometimes intertextuality occurs within the same document, what may be called "local intertextuality." For example, the appearance of the "poor widow" who deposits her whole living into the temple treasury (Mark 12:42) is bound intertextually to the previous passage, in which Jesus warns against religious leaders who "devour widows' houses" (Mark 12:40). Thus, by means of the intertextual correspondence, the "poor widow" is presented not only as an example of true sacrifice, but also as a victim of religious oppression.

Reading Lessons

So, once again Jesus' question comes to the surface. How do we read? The creative and careful biblical preacher will add to the repertoire of biblical methods an attentive eye to narrative dynamics. This task can be intimidating, of course, since few of us have a natural eye for poetic devices and literary patterns. The good news, though, is that the preacher's eye can be trained. Increasingly, biblical commentaries embody literary-critical approaches, and when preachers are guided by these resources to see patterns in narratives, our eye becomes trained to recognize them in other narratives. In other words, the more we see, the more we see; and the more the preacher sees, the more the congregation can hear.

Thomas G. Long is the author of several books on preaching, including The

Witness of Preaching *(Westminster: John Knox, 1988)*. He taught preaching for many years at Princeton Theological Seminary, and he is currently Director of Congregational Resources and Geneva Press at the Presbyterian Publishing Corporation.

NOTES

1. Luke 10:26 (RSV).

2. See, for example, Seymour Chatman, *Story and Discourse: Narrative Structure in Fiction and Film* (Ithaca: N.Y. Cornell University Press, 1978), and Shlomith Rimmon-Kenan, *Narrative Fiction: Contemporary Poetics* (New York: Methuen, 1983).

3. The discussion of the four artistic strategies is an adaptation of material that appeared in Thomas G. Long. "The Biblical Writers as Poets and Artists," in *Proclaim the Gospel,* edited by Cas. J. A. Vos. Privately published at the University of Pretoria, South Africa.

You Will See Angels—Ascending and Descending

Roger Alling

❧

"*Truly, I say to you, you will see the heavens opened and the angels of God ascending and descending on the Son of Man.*" —*John 1:51*

"*We do the works that are of God, along with the Holy Angels.*"—*St. Thomas Aquinas,* Summa Theologica *(cited in Matthew Fox,* Sheer Joy: Conversations with Thomas Aquinas on Creation Spirituality *[San Francisco: Harper SanFrancisco, 1992], 161)*

I

On Sunday we went to the "Glory of Byzantium" exhibit at the Metropolitan Museum of Art. It was a treat. There were angels there... lots of angels. After two hours at the special exhibit, I decided to try an experiment. I went a few floors down to look again at the Western medieval collection to compare it with the Eastern art I had just experienced. I was particularly interested in the respective treatments of the angels.

I found that I had to concentrate my gaze on the Western images. But I had the keen sense that the Eastern images were looking at me. I had to ascend to the realm of the Western angels. The Eastern images, however, seemed to descend toward me, to come in my direction.

"You will see the heavens opened and the angels of God ascending and descending..."

II

A number of years ago I was making some hospital calls on a Friday afternoon. I had just finished my last visit, and was walking down the corridor on my way out the door to the parking lot. Much to my surprise, I took a left-hand turn down another corridor and found myself walking into the hospital room of a complete stranger. Not knowing quite what to say, I introduced myself and asked if there was anything I could do for her. My surprise deepened when she responded with some irritation, "Where have you been? I have been waiting for you for an hour and a half." She had a situation at home that she needed to discuss; and we did so for an hour. When the time came for me to leave, she said, "You have been such an angel today. Thank you for coming!"

I shook my head as I left the hospital and began the process of trying to make sense of what had just happened. "Well, Roger, what did you learn from all that?" I asked.

The first thing I learned was that I didn't fully understand how the visit had taken place. Next, I realized that I did not need to understand. Finally I learned to trust the nudges, hunches, and promptings that come my way.

III

Angels have been out of favor for quite a while, but they seem to be making a comeback. If you go into any large bookstore you will find a whole shelf of current books devoted to the subject. A recent survey indicated that two-thirds of those questioned said that they believe in angels, which is a higher percentage than those who believe that the Social Security system will be there for them when they retire. If you want to be "Touched by an Angel," you tune into a television show of that name each Sunday night.

Often the angels are trivialized in all this material, much as they were in the baroque era when angels were portrayed as little cherub babies.

Ideas that are neglected often return in disguise. I believe that as the religious imagination withdraws from the heavens, science fiction comes and fills the gap. We can see this in the immensely popular *Star Wars* trilogy, and in television shows like the *Third Rock from the Sun*. When the neglected ideas return they do not always do so benignly. Tragedies like the Heaven's Gate suicides occur when the "fiction" in science fiction is forgotten.

Why do these ideas return? What is the issue about angels or about pseudo-angels of the science-fiction substitute? Why do we still seem to care about these things?

Do you remember Albert Einstein's famous reply when he was asked what he thought was the most important intellectual question of his day? His question was this: "Is the Universe friendly or not?"

Is not this something like the question "Is God friendly or not?" Is it like the question about the spirits... "Are they friendly or not?"

IV

Listen again to a portion of today's Gospel as I believe it was first meant to be read.

> *Jesus answered him, "Because I said to you, I saw you under the fig tree, do you believe? You shall see greater things than these." On the third day there was a marriage at Cana in Galilee, and the mother of Jesus was there...*

What did I just do? I left out the verse about the angels. What happens to the story now? What now are the greater things that Nathanael sees?

Nathanael sees the signs of the Fourth Gospel. He sees the miracle of Cana which is the first, with five more to follow which constitute what scholars call the book of signs. This is followed by the greatest sign of all, the account of the passion and resurrection of Jesus.

In other words, Nathanael is promised the vision of the whole Gospel in its Johannine fullness, which is summarized by the evangelist when he writes, "Now Jesus did many other signs in the presence of the disciples, which are not written in this book; but these are written that you may believe that Jesus is the Christ, the Son of God, and that believing you may have life in his name" (John 20:30–31).

This is our answer to Albert Einstein's question about the significant nature of the Universe! Jesus is the Christ, and when we trust him we have life!

One cannot, however, simply move a verse of scripture around without some cause. There are some reasons for believing that John 1:51 did not originally appear at this place in the text, but was a detached saying of Jesus placed in this story by a later editor.

The reasons are these: John only talks about angels after the resurrection account. Pointing directly to the sign at Cana and the other signs is a far more compelling response to Nathanael. In the original language, the "you" in this passage is plural, not singular, as it should be if only Nathanael is being addressed.

V

"You will see the heavens opened and the angels of God ascending and descending on the Son of Man."

We are the ones who are addressed by this saying, not Nathanael! We will see the angels of God ascending and descending.

Ascending and descending: We are pretty good at seeing angels ascending. We know that song by heart. We lift holy hands and hearts to heaven week by week and day by day. "Holy, Holy, Holy...Angels, archangels and all the company of Heaven..."

Angels ascending, visions of the messianic banquet being prepared, the awe and majesty of worship when we do it well; this is all familiar territory for folks like us.

But the angels also descend. This is part of their promise and a part of the help they give. This leads me to the other text I have chosen, one from St. Thomas Aquinas.

> *"We do the works of God along with the Holy Angels"* (Summa Theologica).

The works of God that concern us this week are the preparation and delivery of sermons.

I ask you now to imagine the preacher who is in preparation mode. She has all the raw materials spread before her. She has the scripture, the resources of her own soul and mind. She has the newspaper and its reports, her knowledge of people acquired by experience. She has the needs of the world as she sees them, and the context of the liturgy where her sermon will be offered.

How does it all come together? How does it gel? Is there a nudge, a prodding, a dream, a memory, an insight, an idea, a passion, a tear...? Is there perhaps even a winged echo? Finally, somehow the sermon takes on a shape and comes to life. How?

Perhaps it wasn't all your doing and all your work alone. Perhaps it was the angel you weren't looking for who became the angel looking at you.

Roger Alling is President of the Episcopal Evangelism Foundation and a coeditor of this volume. This sermon was preached on June 4, 1997, on the Propers for the Holy Angels.

HONORING MORAL IMPERATIVES IN THE SPIRITUAL LIFE

Preaching the Good: Homiletics from a Moral Theological Perspective

Thomas Breidenthal

Do moral judgment and preaching go together? In theory, yes. In practice, very seldom. It is tempting to blame this disjuncture on our polarization as a Church, since we disagree passionately about many things. Perhaps it is too risky to name disagreements in the open, let alone to preach about them. But I don't buy that explanation. Any community (of Episcopalians or of others) that has the courage to gather around the Lord's Table Sunday after Sunday has the courage to argue about moral issues. The problem is not in the risk—it lies elsewhere.

We are not afraid of making moral judgments; rather, we think that making moral judgments is immoral. Calling actions right or wrong, good or evil, seems to us disturbingly undemocratic and antipluralistic. Moreover, as Christians we may have been taught to assume that a concern with rules and expectations is positively un-Christian. While the secular world opposes judgment to pluralism, the Christian community often opposes judgment to love. And so, if you are like me, you will do anything to avoid being labeled "judgmental."

I can't speak for the Church as a whole, but I know that at General Seminary, where I teach, there is a thirst for mutual understanding, and a fairly high level of trust. In this respect I do not think General is atypical among Episcopal seminaries. Yet even in the laboratory atmosphere of my course in contemporary Christian ethics, where no one is held accountable outside the classroom for the judgments she has pronounced in the classroom—even there, it is like pulling teeth to get anyone to come down solidly on one side or the other of anything.

Why is this? I think it is because we confuse moral judgment with the attempt to dominate others. Moral theology is theological reflection on acts, practices, policies, and ways of life, with a view to praising them or blaming them. As such, the moral theologian is engaged in the very thing that has given preaching a bad name, and which most of us modern preachers flee from as if from the plague. And no wonder, since often those who claim the moral high ground are devils masquerading as angels. The imposition of power in the name of moral truth, and the exhortation to submission in the name of moral duty, is one of the most successful oppressive strategies the world has known. If we fear allying ourselves with such strategies in the classroom or the refectory, how much more so in the pulpit? How do we use the power of the pulpit appropriately? I am convinced that there is a presumption among preachers in the Episcopal Church, born of a genuine desire not to be abusive, that it is better not to address moral questions directly in sermons; and where this cannot be helped, to avoid engaging in moral argumentation, still less, to express any moral conclusions.

This presumption finds a strong ally in the Reformation conviction that the Gospel is supposed to free us from the dead hand of the law—that is, from the subject of moral theology. Surely the point of the Good News is that we are freed from a preoccupation with judgment, since the moral worth of our lives and the lives of others has been rendered irrelevant by the grace of God in Christ. Judgment has to do with law; and in Christ, so the theory goes, law has been superseded by love.

Understood rightly, this is absolutely true. I believe that Christ has freed us from any preoccupation with the moral life arising from the fear that we must measure up to some standard in order to be accepted by God. If all we did was preach God's unqualified embrace of each of us, it would be enough. Yet I am uncomfortable with the notion that God's law is opposed to God's love. I would rather say that our encounter with God's love in Christ makes possible a new relation to God's law: This relation is the interiorization of God's righteousness and mercy that the Anglican tradition has typically identified with the work of sanctification. The moment we begin to love God as good, and begin to experience God as a person (rather than a mere idea or principle or force), we experience God as law. If this seems counterintuitive, it is because, in our talking about law, we have not yet gotten down to the heart of the matter. We think of law as a demand that presses in on us from outside us. Inevitably, then, we also think of it as something to be resisted. But if we want to know what law means to begin with, we can look, for instance, at Psalm 119: "Your statutes have been like songs to me wherever I have lived as a stranger"; or at Paul, for whom the perfect law of God is no less perfect for our inability to fulfill it (Romans 7:12). For Richard Hooker, who might justly be called the founder of Anglican moral theology, law is the patterned beauty of God, finding expression in the orderly disposition of the universe, and in the hunger for wisdom that drives the human heart and mind. Commenting on Romans 2:14, Hooker writes:

> *They are a law unto themselves. [Paul's] meaning is, that by force of the light of reason, wherewith God illuminateth everyone which cometh into the world, men being enabled to know truth from falsehood, and good from evil, do thereby learn in many things what the will of God is; which will himself not revealing by any extraordinary means unto them, but they by natural discourse attaining the knowledge thereof, seem the makers of those laws which indeed are his, and they but only the finders of them out.* (Laws of Ecclesiastical Polity, Bk. 1:8)

No dry linearity this, but the knobbly, fractal, unpredictable but profoundly orderly exfoliation of a reality that coheres, that goes together, that calls out for the poet's naming. When we recognize this we move from terror of law to love of God: from the terror that so often attends our initial encounters with God, to a confidence and gratitude arising from the intuition that God in God's lawfulness is trustworthy and never arbitrary. Beginning with Hooker, this insistence on the lawfulness, as opposed to the sovereignty, of God has distinguished Anglicanism from Calvinism. In God's law we find our own true calling, the ground of our own freedom. The law is not essentially a stranger, but the key to my own existence, my own true self.

Only when we acknowledge the "fit" between us and the law can we appreciate what is implied in the fact that the law so often seems a stranger or even an enemy. The law becomes our enemy when we want to do things which run contrary to it. But if Paul and Hooker are right, every such act runs contrary to our own good as well. Thus, when we disobey the law, we are also turning against ourselves. Viewed in this way, the law is not an external force, opposed to our will, but something planted within us. It is the principle of our own being, crying out on our own behalf when we transgress it. In the same way, when we speak of things we "should" or "ought to" do, we are not referring to agendas imposed on us from outside, but are pointing to courses of action which, however painful, are most in keeping with our true dignity as human beings and children of God. At the same time, of course, "should" and "ought" express our resistance to a given course of action: this is the burden of words like "ought" and "should," of concepts like obligation and duty. If I truly wanted to do the right thing, I would not feel it as my duty to do it. When I experience a sense of obligation, this is a sure sign that my will is divided. This is precisely what Paul is talking about when he says "I do not do the good I want, but the evil I do not want is what I do" (Romans 7:19). It is precisely where I feel obligation and duty that I encounter my own inner resistance to the law—a resistance which stands in opposition to my own desire to fulfill the law spontaneously.

Some will argue that the Pauline crisis is not everybody's crisis. But making allowance for personality types, and maybe even for gender differences, I think that even those who do not experience the gap between the law and the will as a crisis, experience it as an ache. In any case, the situation is untenable. Either my heart must be released, or the law must be abandoned. And then we are back either to terror in the face of the divine command or to the dullness of spirit with which most of us protect ourselves from terror.

Christian theology finds its wellspring in the freedom Christ brings us from this untenable situation. We begin by proclaiming that whatever we have failed to do by way of righteousness, Jesus has done for us. Some would say this is enough: Any talk about morality at this point will only blunt the sharp edge of the Good News. But if "should" and "ought" really do have to do with our fulfillment as children of God, the moral struggle is not so much something to be set aside in Christ, as it is something to be taken up again with renewed hope. Christ has given us the spiritual leisure to return to the places of obligation, to our marriages, our roles as parents or adult children, our work, our affliction or weakness, in order that, in so doing, we may begin to own our true dignity as followers of the One who died and rose for us. Obligation must be turned into habit, habit into virtue, virtue into character.

This is where preaching comes in. First and foremost, good preaching convinces us that God loves us and that Jesus has already claimed us as his own. But preaching can and should go further, by teasing out the situations which confront us with obligation, and in so doing alerting us to the places where we are resisting the kingdom of God. With this in mind, I offer the following proposals for your consideration.

1. Don't avoid the topic of God's law. I chose to entitle this talk "Preaching the Good" rather than "Preaching the Good News," because I think we sometimes forget that the very term "Good News" loses its meaning unless we have some notion what we consider goodness in itself to be. The biblical tradition grounds the notion of goodness in the lawfulness of God. When you preach, then, do not neglect to talk about God's law. Explore how it confronts us in our weakness and sinfulness as external demand. Honor the mystery of Christ as the

manifestation of God's law in humankind. Stir up in yourself and in your hearers the longing of the psalmist for the sweetness of a law so humane we yearn to live by it.

2. Do not shrink from naming and exploring the areas of life where there are duties and obligations to be addressed—either in order that they may be rejected or clarified, or that they may be owned up to and taken on. We need to name the issues that divide and trouble us: abortion, same-sex unions, capital punishment, the place of religion in the schools and in public life, the rights of immigrants, the moral limits of the free market, the legalization of euthanasia, to name just a few. We do not need to provide authoritative answers, but we need publicly to frame questions in the light of the Gospel, so that permission is given to argue, study, pray, and witness about the moral life.

3. Try to make the connections between biblical texts, Christian doctrines, and moral life. Theological reflection leads almost immediately to moral reflection. But in sermons the best theological reflection often stops at the threshold of Christian ethics and goes no further. Sometimes there simply isn't time. But where there is a strong tradition of preaching from Sunday to Sunday, by one or more preachers well known to the congregation and trusted by them, there is no reason why some sermons, at least, shouldn't start with ethics and work back.

4. Finally, don't be afraid to state your own moral judgment on a given matter. We must not abuse the power of the pulpit, but a conviction thought through, prayed about, and plainly argued will only squelch free moral discourse if it is part of a larger pattern of domination. Better to make a moral claim that is wrong, than through fear of being wrong or stepping on people's toes to model a refusal to make moral judgments at any time. I am reminded of André Trocmé, the Protestant pastor of the French village of Le Chambon, who demanded from the pulpit that his congregation not cooperate with the Vichy regime in its attempt to locate and register Jews. As a result of his preaching and his example, the people of Le Chambon went on to rescue and hide five thousand Jews—as many Jews as there were villagers.

In calling for a deeper theological engagement with the law of God, I do not seek to make us a more moralistic people. God knows we are moralistic enough already. We Anglicans especially have always been eager to settle for good order, due process, and the settling of disputes on technicalities. Legalism, not wishy-washiness, is the historical vice of our tradition. I am not interested in formulating rules and reminding others about them. I am interested, rather, in learning how we might better submit to the easy yoke of Jesus. Even when our texts do not call for explicit moral reflection, it is our duty as preachers to keep the moral landscape in view, to bring to life those touchstones of the Christian experience that make a moral discourse grounded in the certainty of salvation and inclusivity possible. Let us preach the strangeness of God, the beauty and terror of God's law, the ache of our longing to receive hearts of flesh rather than stone. In so doing, we will do our part to assist in the painful but absolutely hopeful work of assessment and amendment that marks the Christian life.

Thomas Breidenthal is Associate Professor of Moral Theology at The General Theological Seminary in New York.

Standing Out of the Way of the Gospel: The Martyrs of Lyons

Joe G. Burnett
1 Peter 1:3–9; Mark 8:34–38

I

Who could not be moved by the story of the martyrs of Lyons? According to the graphic account of Eusebius, several members of Christian households—Sanctus, Attalus, Marturus, Pothinus, and Blandina—who valiantly denied the false accusations being hurled against believers in the mid-second century were beaten, tortured with red-hot irons, and mauled by wild beasts in a public spectacle. Blandina was so filled with power to withstand these assaults that she exhausted her torturers: "I am a Christian," she cried, "and nothing vile is done among us."

When all the others had been slain, she was "beaten, torn, and burned with irons," then "wrapped in a net and tossed about by a wild bull. The spectators were amazed at her endurance."

I am amazed. But I am also terrified. Such stories bring back long-buried memories of Sunday evening church services in small-town Mississippi Methodist congregations where I grew up. Sunday nights were ripe for life-changing rededications. I recall sitting there, listening to passionate preaching, swept along in the spirit's current. I was a baptized Christian, but on Sunday nights I gave my heart to Jesus—again, and again, and again.

In the midst of my zeal I feared but one thing—the call to missionary service. I had sat through the testimonies of these envoys who periodically returned to raise money for their enterprise. I had watched their Kodachrome slides depicting the squalor and poverty that was their daily challenge. And I had heard the recent reports of a team of Christian missionaries savagely ambushed in some foreign jungle—run through with spears, for God's sake! I would sing fervently,

> *Have thine own way, Lord, have thine own way;*
> *Thou art the potter, I am the clay.*
> *Mold me and make me after thy will,*
> *while I am waiting, yielded and still.*[1]

But then I would add a silent, anxious prayer: "Lord, I am yours; mold me, and make me your disciple. But…if you can find it in your gracious will for my life, please let me serve and love you right here at home!

II

There are conflicting temptations that confront us as preachers: The first is the lure of the moments of high drama in our great tradition. If we can lift up some heroic example like Blandina, or if we can train the spotlight on some transfiguring encounter from the New Testament, then maybe we can write large the Gospel's claim across the screens of our congregants' minds. We can appeal to them to make a vow, to take a stand, to do or die, or even to become missionaries!

Mark's Jesus seems ready to do just that. He's in no mood to mince words. His call is swift and sharp. "If any"—he calls the whole crowd around, not just the disciples— "If any want to become my followers, let them deny themselves and take up their cross and follow me."

Sound familiar? Sound like some of our more adversarial preaching? It's now or never! You're with me or you're against me! Get on the road to Jerusalem, or get off!

The danger is that we will scare away lots of people who can't fathom how on earth their obedience can ever measure up. Or, that after so much sermonic pounding we will simply deaden their senses and they will turn us off completely.

Recently the *New York Times* was full of letters to the editor from people who jumped with both feet on the case of a local rabbi, who had recently written to complain of ministerial burnout. One after another took his "liberal clergy" mentality to task, or decried his blaming the congregation or society for his troubles, or dismissed his gripes about low pay. The comment that really struck a nerve came from a Florida woman: "I sympathize with [the rabbi]," she wrote, "but members of the clergy have abused their position in front of captive audiences, and are suffering the consequences. Why I remember one Roman Catholic ceremony where, in the middle of a lovely marriage service, the priest began his homily by addressing the couple with: 'You think you're pretty smart, don't you?'"

Mark's Jesus does that too. "You think you're pretty smart, don't you?" he says to his readers. "Get this: The Jesus of your faith is no highly exalted master, but a suffering servant. It's the crucified one who says to you, 'Those who want to save their life will lose it, and those who lose their life for my sake, and for the sake of the Gospel, will save it.'" In a world where the church is increasingly persecuted, and where—if some scholars are correct—the temple has already been destroyed, Mark sounds a solemn, unequivocal warning.

The question for us preachers is, are we called to say it as Mark said it? Acutely conscious as we are of the urgency of the Gospel, must we lace our sermons with the bitter ingredient, "You think you're pretty smart, don't you?" Or is there another way?

I will never forget the cautionary words of a trusted mentor in the Hebrew scriptures: "Do not pretend to preach the prophets," he warned his students, "for if you truly succeed in casting their message in homiletic terms, you will empty your churches. If, however, you hold back, and fail to do the prophets justice, you will compromise their gospel beyond recognition."

III

That latter warning is, I believe, the essence of the second temptation that faces all preachers. It is the temptation to water down and accommodate the message in order to make it more enthralling or merely feasible. The writer of the first letter of Peter might have been tempted to do that. Later in Mark's generation, the church has become marginalized by a pagan culture. The believers are "resident aliens," routinely abused because their faith calls them to break with the social fabric of their communities. This writer does not give in, does not yield to the temptation to minimize their present suffering in the light of some future reward, but links their pain to the passion of Christ: "In this you rejoice," the writer says, "even if now for a little while you have had to suffer various trials...."

I wonder—nearly a hundred years later—could a Sanctus or an Attalus or a Marturus or a Pothinus or a Blandina been as ready to face their agony had the writer of this epistle simply said "Don't worry, be happy"? Surely there is another way.

At the insistence of many of my parishioners, I recently began reading *At Home in Mitford,* the first in a popular series by author Jan Karon chronicling the ministry of a fictional Episcopal priest named Father Tim in a small town in the high country of North Carolina. In the early chapters, Fr. Tim receives a surprise visit from the lovely, sophisticated— and wealthy—Olivia Davenport.

"Father Tim," she said, as she crossed her shapely legs, "I'm dying."

He hoped his face didn't convey the shock he felt.

"I'm asking you to help me find something to make the rest of my life worth living."

Olivia Davenport goes on to tell of her winter and summer homes, left to her by her mother. She confesses that though she is tempted to spend her last months being quite idle and carefree, "I did not come to Mitford to join the club and sit by the pool."

"I want to do something that will make a difference," she concludes. "I don't know what that something is, but I believe with all my heart that you can tell me."

In the brief conversation that follows, the rector is stunned by a sense of the Spirit's presence. Before many moments have passed, he has led this elegant, now broken and frightened woman to a simple, long needed, and life-giving community service—reading to other dying patients at the local hospital.

Karon writes: "In the space of precisely seven minutes, which he reckoned to be the full length of her visit, he had been told a terrible truth, discovered an answer to prayer, helped someone find a ministry, and been unutterably refreshed in his own spirit. Perhaps, he thought, we should all live as if we're dying."

IV

Perhaps we should all live as if we're dying.

Here, I suggest, is a clue to the kind of preaching that can expose hearts and change lives: not in the haughty words of prophetic pretension, and not in the easy words that belie bottomless hypocrisy, but in a daily dying to self in pulpit and in parish. Here is the context for a genuine expository preaching that can preserve and explore the capacity to confront the powers, as well as offer comfort to those who have no power.

Look at Mark's Gospel. Where are the high moments of transformation and conversion? Where is it that disciples are summoned, and shaped, and sent? Is it not "on the way"? Time and again we are peppered with that phrase—on the way, on the way, on the way. There is where the conversations take place, the unfaithfulness is rebuked, the decisions are made, and the strong bonds of faith are forged. In Mark's story of Jesus, the community of disciples lives and loves and loses on the way.

Where exactly is "on the way" in our world? Is it not in and among the places and people we serve as priests, pastors, and preachers? And what does it mean for we preachers to deny ourselves, and take up our cross, and follow Jesus on that way? What does it mean for us to lose our lives for his sake and the Gospel's, in order to save them?

In volume two of Karon's series, *A Light in the Window*, Mitford's rector takes an extended vacation following a diabetic coma. He leaves the sacramental services in the hands of a supply, but, to the astonishment of his flock, he entrusts the preaching to a rural Baptist minister named Absalom Greer.

"I'll preach the cross," Absalom warns, as if to threaten heresy, "and redemption by the blood."

Fr. Tim responds, "You'll be a tough act to follow."

Upon his return, with the congregation slightly baffled but still intact, he congratulates the aging evangelist: "God bless you for all the effort you gave us here.... [A parishioner] told me you were as plain as the bark on a tree."

Absalom replies: We have to "stand out of the way of the Gospel, and that keeps us plain if we let it."

How much we preachers need to learn to stand out of the way of the Gospel! How much we need to remember what keeps us plain; to resist the urge to say too much or too little—to border on the trite, or to lose our listeners in needless complexity.

Barbara Brown Taylor is right. It is a preaching life. It is all of a piece, a coherent whole. It has something to do with holiness of life, but more to do with personal authenticity. It has something to do with emotion, but more to do with conviction. It has something to do with scholarship, but more to do with sound reason. It has something to do with gumption and "guts," but more to do with grace. It has something to do with self-affirmation, but much more to do with self-surrender.

Chances are most of us—indeed, most of our people—will never be called upon to endure the red-hot irons that tormented Blandina. Yet the eloquence of our witness, if we are faithful, will be determined by countless small acts of heroism and hope. At its best, our preaching is one of those acts. It is a sacramental act, a great homiletic fraction anthem, a breaking of the word, a little martyrdom—often undertaken with people who know they are dying, and who want to make a difference, and who believe with all their hearts that we can tell them how.

Yes, we preachers are part of a public spectacle. The pulpit is the "net" in which we are tossed about. The "wild beasts" are the temptations that draw us from plainspoken, loving truth. Our congregants are our fellow "captives." Day and night, in a succession of little life and death moments "on the way," they all wait and watch and listen with bated breath. They want to know if we have gotten over our fear of being missionaries. They watch to see if we will stay on the road with Jesus. They listen to hear if we will go on saying, "I am a Christian!" And they wonder: Can we stand out of the way of the Gospel?

Joe G. Burnett is rector of Trinity Episcopal Church in Hattiesburg, Mississippi.

NOTES

1. *Lesser Feasts and Fasts.* New York: The Church Hymnal Corporation, 1988, 246.

CELEBRATING THE TREASURES IN A FAITH TRADITION

Preaching from the *Via Media*:
Pursuing an Anglican Style of Address

Mitties McDonald DeChamplain

I have come to believe that all of us at one time or another are haunted by images of what I call the "virtuoso performance" model of preaching—the dazzling, dynamic, powerful, eloquent pulpiteers which so many in our congregations still associate with true preaching excellence. The virtuoso performance model, and all the perfectionistic images associated with it, can be disabling and inhibiting to budding preachers who are laboring to find their own authentic pulpit styles. I also suspect that many seasoned preachers have at least occasionally to wrestle with images within which tyrannize.

In search of liberating images to sustain us in our quest for excellence, I am convinced that we must look to the received wisdom of our Prayer Book tradition in shaping our vision of preaching. This is not exactly a remarkable assertion on my part; and much of what I have to say will strike observant Episcopal seminarians as "sanctified common sense." Still, it is common sense that needs reaffirmation in contexts like this Preaching Excellence Program, where we are intentionally gathered to reinvigorate our understanding and practice of preaching.

Consider first my conviction that there is a whole theology of preaching encapsulated in one of the prayers for mission appointed for optional use in Morning Prayer II:

> *Lord Jesus Christ, you stretched out your arms of love on the hard wood of the cross that everyone might come within the reach of your saving embrace: So clothe us in your Spirit that we, reaching forth our hands in love, may bring those who do not know you to the knowledge and love of you; for the honor of your Name.*[1]

For me this collect is a central, controlling image by which we Anglican preachers ought to discern both what to say and how to be in the pulpit. The prayer is, as I see it, a homiletical mission statement. And its cruciform image of embrace is a vivid reminder that when we are preaching sermons, we are seeking to make communion an encounter between the Good News of the Gospel and the people of God through verbal and nonverbal symbol. Our strategies for making sermons need to be strategies of embrace. Our language must be the language of love, a way of expression that reveals God's eternal good will toward people. To say that ours must be a language of love and embrace is not to suggest that we are in the business of making our congregations feel good all the time. I am instead referring to love in its deeper and more powerful sense, summarized beautifully by John Macquarrie in the *Principles of Christian Theology*:

> *Love, in its ontological sense, is letting-be. Love usually gets defined in terms of union, or the drive toward union, but such a definition is too egocentric. Love does indeed lead to community, but to aim primarily at uniting the other person to oneself, or oneself to him, is not the secret of love and may even be destructive of genuine community. Love is letting-be, not, of course, in the sense of standing off from someone or something, but in the positive and active sense of enabling-to-be. When we talk of "letting-be," we are to understand both parts of this hyphenated expression in a strong sense—"letting" as "empowering," and "be" as enjoying the maximal range of being that is open to the particular being concerned. Most typically, "letting-be" means helping a person into the full realization of his [or her] potentialities for being.*[2]

To preach the truth in love will require of each of us to use all that there is to use to enable the people of God to see the vivid, graphic, demanding, potent nature of the saving story of Jesus Christ.

With the image of "saving embrace" as our foundation, the next question is, "What else is distinctive about Anglican preaching?" It is conceivable that not a long list of ready answers may come immediately to mind. The Episcopal Church is not exactly known for its spellbinding sermons. An amusing reflection comes from Walker Percy in his book *The Second Coming*. "The main virtue of Episcopalians" he observes, "is their gift for reticence. Seldom can an Episcopalian (or an Anglican) be taken for a Christian. Perhaps that is what I like about them. A mystery: If the good news is true, why...is the proclamation itself such a weary used-up thing"?[3]

Now, I want to be bold to say, in spite of Percy's observation about Anglican "reticence," I believe that, in a world brimming with angry fundamentalists and radicals, our fabled reticence is mostly a good thing. It enables us to walk the *via media* between theological extremes. Reticence may well be a key characteristic for those of us who want to renew our commitment to excellence in preaching, as long as the reticence does not deteriorate into "fence straddling." And so, before I outline what I believe to be five key attributes of the Anglican way of preaching, let me say a word or two about the *via media*. In our time, I think the *via media* is no longer just the "middle way" between Catholic and Protestant but is also the middle way between the polarized religious groups of today's world. Alister McGrath makes note of this in his book *The Renewal of Anglicanism*:

> *There is a real need for the reconstruction of the via media that avoids the increasingly outmoded dialectic between "Catholic" and "Protestant" and addresses the real issue of today: the failure of both liberalism and fundamentalism to provide a relevant and responsible form of Christianity for today's world. One collapses into the world, the other refuses to have anything to do with it. If ever a via media was needed, it is now. As Hans Küng pointed out recently, the church "must find a way between a modernism without foundations and a fundamentalism without modernity. Anglicanism is poised to provide exactly such a middle way"...Anglicanism already possesses a concern both for the fundamentals of the faith, without being "fundamentalist," and for generous toleration, without being "liberal," as those two terms are now widely understood.*[4]

The "middle way" suggested by McGrath reminds me that ours is a bridge-building church, and its preachers are among the primary bridge builders. We seek through the media of symbol, voice, and body to unify and reconcile extremes. This brings me to the first attribute or distinctive of our style of address: Anglican preaching has a tolerance for ambiguity. Anglicanism at its best has always been willing to live with and love the hard questions of the faith, while standing firmly anchored in Tradition. We openly accept what Bishop Rowan Williams calls "the intractable strangeness of the ground of belief," the many ways in which God remains ever mysterious to the human mind. We also know that genuine faith cannot flourish in an environment where doubt is not honored and understood as an inevitable part of each person's faith journey. Anglican preachers must take doubt seriously when engaging biblical texts and the people of God. This means, at the very least, we will be reluctant in our preaching to tie up hard questions with a fancy bow, and present them to the congregation in a long list of sparkling and tidy answers. "Superficial cheerfulness" in our address is not a satisfying way of encouraging people to "be of good cheer." We must avoid impulses to fix up or to bypass hard sayings in scripture and hard times in people's lives. Because we preach "Christ crucified," we believe that there is a decisive reply to the problem of evil in the world, even if there are no answers. The cross stands as a perpetual reminder that, supremely in our difficulties in life, God is with us. While we must boldly and unapologetically proclaim "that all things necessary to salvation" are contained in scripture, we also acknowledge that God and the Good News are never confined there. Scripture preached with fidelity and competence will, by the grace of God, lead us into ever deepening recognition of the mystery that God is—with confidence that God is. We are thus content to live in tension with texts and contexts, always wrestling to find a life-giving word of truth from God which speaks directly to the pressing concerns of our congregations and our world.

Closely related to the first attribute is a second: Anglican preaching is provisional. Anglican preaching at its best is always marked by being open-minded and receptive to ideas that might require adjustment. In *The Future of Anglicanism*, it is explained that "the provisional denotes the condition of innovation, of continual creation, of presence in changing situations: It is opposed to a stubborn concern to stop the moment, the mobility of forms or the mortality of relationships."[5] What this implies for us as preachers is that we take our positions firmly without being dogmatic. We are noncoercive in our strategies of pulpit address—open-handed instead of closed-fisted in style. I want to recall at this point a moment in the wonderful address of the Reverend Elizabeth Templeton to the 1988 Lambeth Conference. In her remarks she congratulated the Anglican Communion for what she called its "blessed generosity across parties, camps, styles, and dogma. Internally and in relation to other evolving Christian life-forms, [she said,] you are conspicuously unclassifiable—a kind of ecclesiastical duck-billed platypus." Templeton went on to assure the bishops that our "remarkable openness of being is to be celebrated and not deplored. [Our] costly openness is a gift to other churches and a gift to the world."

The third attribute that I will mention will not surprise you in the least: Anglican preaching is liturgical in its shape and character. It really does make a difference to our preaching that its matrix is most commonly the Eucharist. Many of the nuances and presuppositions that we need in interpreting the texts on which our sermons are based grow out of the liturgy. Whenever I prepare to study a set of propers, I always look at the Prayer Book and Hymnal as my first commentaries for sermon preparation. They are wonderful exegetical tools in their own right. In his classic monograph on *What Is Liturgical Preaching?* Reginald Fuller sounded a keynote for us all by asserting that "the purpose of the liturgical sermon is to renew in the individual members the sense that they are members of the ecclesia.... The sermon acts as a bridge between Baptism and Eucharist...; it is the function of the liturgical sermon to reach back to the Baptism of the members of the congregation, to renew in them the sense of membership of the ecclesia, and to lead forward to the liturgical action of the Eucharist." The upshot of Fuller's essay is that Anglican preachers must, in their preparation, continuously study the Word "as that Word is expressed in the Liturgy. [They] must...constantly live in the Liturgy, in its daily round of offices and frequent celebration of the Eucharist, in the yearly cycle of feast and fast. Thus will [they] learn to bring every thought into captivity to the obedience of Christ."[6] The Prayer Book forms us and conditions our preaching reflexes for fitting response to each occasion.

This, of course, leads us to a fourth consideration: Anglican preaching is deeply Incarnational. Just as we make Eucharist week after week in the belief that Christ's real presence is in the consecrated bread and wine, so we also hear the Gospel proclaimed in the hope that the invisible God revealed to us in Jesus Christ will be made really present in the sacrament of the words preached. We openly acknowledge that words, like the consecrated bread and wine, can feed and enable us to "taste and see that the Lord is good." The faithful re-presentation of the Jesus story week after week in a lively and glowing manner paves the way for the faithful to encounter the divine. Each and every sermon will, implicitly or explicitly, have a christological center. I like to think that our very incarnational image of "saving embrace"—deeply rooted as it is in the earthing of God for us—is suggestive of a way of preaching that is more devoted to invitation than exhortation, more invested in fleshing out indicatives than drawing out imperatives. We want our sermons to make the True Human Being known in ways that lead people into ever deepening relationship with the Christ whose image we are to become in the world.

I think that these four attributes point naturally to a fifth distinctive: Anglican preaching is committed to telling the whole truth. Now I do not mean to suggest that preachers from other denominations have no care for the truth; but I do mean to stress the very Catholic nature of the Anglican commitment to truth telling. We own the whole of life in the pulpit, admitting to both its tragic and comic peculiarities, holding "lament and praise" in ever deepening tension.

Rowan Williams puts it well when he says that the Catholic approach "keeps nothing back, leaves nothing out that could contribute to our healing. Ours is not a faith in which some things are carefully reserved for the élite, but one in which truth is public and accessible, in which people are trusted to be allowed to approach God as God is, not held at arm's length by professionals dealing out carefully rationed quantities of information.... This is not a faith for specialists, but opens up something for all. Neither we nor God have to be protected from each other."[7]

To round out these reflections, I can point enthusiastically to two practical implications. The first is that in our verbal style, we must be painstakingly devoted to finding "lively and glowing" images to flesh out the concepts we address. Anglican preaching will have a special rhetorical reverence for the sermon as a Speech Act (an oral/aural event), and this demands of us that our remarks possess "instant intelligibility" for the ear of the listener. We will naturally condition our reflexes to use more synonymous words, more amplifying phrases, more re-statement in crafting sermons which readily can be heard and understood. We honor the ears of the listener in address, and we are thus generous in our use of concrete, imaginative, and evocative language.

A second implication of my thinking is that all Anglican preachers will have a commitment to the Natural Delivery, which, put in incarnational terms, means fully embodied presentational style. The Natural School of delivery, of course, was given its most eloquent expression by the Anglican Archbishop of Dublin, Richard Whately, in 1828:

> *The practical rule then to be adopted...is, not only to pay no studied attention to the Voice, but studiously to withdraw the thoughts from it, and to dwell as intently as possible on the Sense; trusting to nature to suggest spontaneously the proper emphases and tones.*[8]

These are liberating words for those who are trying to find their preaching voice and their own particular pulpit manner. Whately's words are a call to forget about the voice and the body at the moment of utterance and to be obedient to and abandoned within our subject matter when we speak. It is a summons to unselfconsciousness while preaching. For this is when the voice and body are likely to respond with greatest authenticity. The invitation in the end is to be who we are in the pulpit; to condition our reflexes where they need it; and then to forget about everything except the message when we preach. It is consistent with our image of "saving embrace" to say that I think of preaching ultimately as an act of self-offering, which happens at its best when we are self-forgetful in the action of preaching.

Mitties McDonald DeChamplain is Associate Professor of Preaching and Communication Studies at Fuller Theological Seminary.

NOTES

1. *The Book of Common Prayer*, 101.

2. John Macquarrie, *Principles of Christion Theology*, 2d ed. (New York: Charles Scribner's Sons, 1977), 348–49.

3. Walker Percy, *The Second Coming* (New York: Farrar, Stratus and Giroux, 1980), 189–90.

4. Alister E. McGrath, *The Renewal of Anglicanism* (Harrisburg, Pa.: Morehouse Publishing, 1993), 110–11.

5. Robert Hannaford, ed., *The Future of Anglicanism* (Herefordshire, England: Gracewing, 1996), 6.

6. Reginald H. Fuller, *What is Liturgical Preaching?* (London: SCM Press, 1957), 12, 57.

7. Rowan Williams, "Teaching the Truth," in *Living Tradition: Affirming Catholicism in the Anglican Church*, edited by Jeffrey John (Cambridge, Mass.: Cowley Publications, 1992), 30.

8. Excerpt found in James L. Golden and Edward P. J. Corbett, eds., *The Rhetoric of Blair, Campbell, and Whately* (New York: Holt, Rinehart and Winston, 1968), 383.

Comfort, Credibility, and Credentials

Neil Alexander

Rewind your tape to grade school. Your teacher reaches into the desk drawer and gets the lanyard with the whistle, then reaches into the closet and retrieves the large, red rubber kickball. The class makes a perfect line at the door. Everyone makes an exit to the playground. With every step the anticipation builds.

At the playground it is time to choose up sides; and the teacher points to two of the unlikeliest schoolmates to be captains of the team. You wait for the "choosing ritual" to begin, and the excitement of the previous moment turns to panic. "Oh no," you say to yourself. "Will I be chosen by the best team? Will I be chosen near the beginning? Will I be chosen at all?" As the team begins to take shape, your anxiety turns another somersault. One team already looks stronger than the other and you say to yourself, "Kickball is not really my game anyway. If I end up on the weak team, maybe they won't expect too much of me. If I get chosen by the winning team, I just might have to produce."

I get that same sort of pit-in-the-stomach anxiety every time I read the opening verses of Luke 10. The Lord appoints seventy—and that's all of us—the Church, not some special cadre of disciples, and sends them out two-by-two.

I did an informal survey last week. I asked a number of preachers and nonpreachers about their first impressions about this text. They all agreed that the first thing that strikes them is the comfort factor of being sent out together, comfort in the fact that we are not alone in being sent. Two-by-two means I will not be alone; I'll be out there as a laborer in the harvest, but I will not be alone.

It is certainly possible to hear that as good news, but playground pit-in-the-stomach panic runs all over me. When I go out there and labor in the vineyard of the Lord I want to pick my harvesting partner! When the day gets long I want to be with someone who will refresh me on my terms. When the talk turns to politics I want someone who will agree with me. When the time comes to turn in the fruits of the harvest I want someone with the same sense of justice. Okay, I understand the part about being sent as a lamb in the midst of wolves; but can't I at least go with someone I like, someone I trust, someone who is concerned for my well-being? Can I accept it if I am sent, and my partner in the procession is the homeless man up the street who hasn't bathed in weeks? Can I accept it if I am sent and my partner in the procession is red, or yellow, or black, or brown, or white? Can I accept it if I am sent and my partner in the procession is an Anglo-Catholic, or an evangelical, a liberal, or a conservative?

Okay, I understand that you are sure that you can handle it no matter who you're paired off with; but can they handle you—just as you are? Man, woman, young, old, gay, straight, Gregorian chant, gospel rap? Things are much easier when two-by-two is comforting, when your partner is your refuge. But two-by-two is not about comfort, it is about credibility. Paul and Barnabas, Peter and John, Barnabas and Mark, Paul and Silas—these must surely have enjoyed each other's company. Surely they must have found comfort and security in being together. But the Mosaic Law required two witnesses for the testimony to be credible.

We move together in mission not for ourselves, but for the sake of the Gospel. We are sent together into the vineyard because the difference in our perspectives, the diversity of our passions, the variety of our experiences thicken and enrich and intensify and bring credibility to our witness in the Name of Jesus.

A friend of mine has suggested that in the Church we need to think of the word "together" not as an adverb, but as a noun. Acting together, living together, being together, working together—no sense of together is as important as simply being a together, that mysterious together of souls and bodies that belong to each other because they all belong to God.

In a few short weeks our Church will gather in General Convention. It is an important time—the election of a new presiding bishop to be our chief pastor and set the tone of our mission and ministry in the next decade. The Lutheran-Episcopal Concordat is potentially the most important ecumenical moment since John XXIII called Vatican II into session. Then there are the canonical matters to be decided on the ordination of women and the memorials from dioceses asking for an official liturgical rite for the blessing of same-sex unions. Much will happen in Philadelphia; some of it exciting; some of it potentially divisive; and in every case the world will be watching—vigilant to test the integrity of our witness. Many will work hard to push through their party platform, or achieve an ideological victory, or win the day on some issue that will preserve the Church faithful, true, and bold. And if we are not careful, it will have all been about our own need for comfort and security in the face of the imperatives of the Gospel; and it will all have been at the expense of the credibility of our witness to Jesus.

In the ancient world, rulers would send emissaries—ambassadors—to neighboring regions. According to the custom of the day, reflected in today's Gospel, the emissary would carry no provisions, minimal clothing, no weapon for personal safety; they would take with them only their diplomatic credentials. And that was not a passport or document, but usually a stone or a piece of wood that bore the seal of the one they represented. The seal they carried with them and all the power that stood behind it was the single most important factor in accomplishing the mission for which they had been sent. Nothing else was required; anything else got in the way.

"You are sealed with the Holy Spirit in Baptism and marked as Christ's own forever." "All newborn soldiers of the Crucified bear on their brow the seal of him who died." Being chosen and sent can still today feel much like it did those warm spring mornings on the grade-school playground. We will still have to worry about the Lord's choices for our harvesting partners; can we accept them? Will they accept us? We will still have to struggle with the differences in how God has made us, how God is calling us, how God is transforming us in ways we cannot ask or imagine. But our credentials are secure: sealed, marked, forever.

The Reverend Canon J. Neil Alexander, Th.D., is Professor of Homiletics in the School of Theology of the University of the South, Sewanee, Tennessee.

Accessing the Energy in an Oral Art

Stick It in Your Ear! Preaching as an Oral-Aural Transaction

Neil Alexander

Someone once attributed to Martin Luther the delightful quip, "Christianity is a Word and someone has to stick it in your ear!" I've searched a fair cross section of Luther's writings trying to find the context for that line and for the German phrase for which it must surely be a loose translation. In any event, it is the sort of thing he would say (it is entirely consistent with his theology of the living word) and closely related to another image for which he is well known.

The church, Luther said, is a "mouth house," not a "pen house."[1] He was making a couple of important points. First, Luther was suggesting that the living Word of God was a word preached by way of a human being to a gathered congregation of God's faithful folk. In other words, one understanding of the Word of God takes the form of a dynamic transaction between God and God's people by way of the living voice of the preacher. Luther was also reminding us of something else with his use of this image: The church had a witness, a Preached Word, before there was a collection of sacred scriptures. The *viva vox evangeli*—the living voice of the Gospel—was the precious treasure of the church that called together a community of faith in the Name of Jesus. The church proclaimed Christ crucified, risen, and coming again before it had a text. The church had a Word of the Risen Savior before it had a book.

There are many implications of this for the work of preaching. Luther's image forces us to consider the nature of preaching itself. When we preach are we participating in an interhuman conversation—talk among people (even if about something as important as the resurrection of Jesus)—or are we active participants in a divine-human transaction of sacred speech? Are we simply talking about God (or salvation, or eternity, or whatever) or are we captured by the vital sense of living word so visible on the pages of scripture that it is impossible to distinguish speech and action? "Let there be light!" declared God, "and there was light," records the writer of Genesis. God spoke and it was done; it was done by speaking! Luther's image helps us contemplate the nature of what it means to preach.

If we take Luther's image one step further, we must ask the question, "What are we to preach?" What was the Preached Word of the Church—the apostolic preaching—before the Church collected the body of sacred texts we know as the New Testament? What was the sacred word before the sacred texts? What was in circulation "mouth-to-mouth" before it was in circulation on the written page? What was the news, teeming with the power of the Spirit, that called the faith community into being? Most of us would say that "the news" was Jesus of Nazareth who was crucified, died, buried, risen, ascended, and coming again. That's the news! Nothing more, nothing less. And the sacred texts that live at the center of the Church's life are the record of all the head-scratching that went on in the apostolic communities about what they were going to do in response to that news. Capturing this dimension of Luther's image for preaching is incredibly important. It goes right to the question of the content of our preaching—not the what, but the Who. The Sunday eucharistic assembly pulsates with an eschatological energy that pulls us toward God's future, and as preachers we stand between the font and the altar to preach Jesus Christ, to preach the news that was before the text.

At this point you might be wondering if I am reducing the role of scripture in preaching. Absolutely not! Far from it. In fact, when preaching focuses more clearly on "the news," then it is possible to break open the texts with a fresh alertness to their message. The New Testament, for example, gives us inspired insight into the what of Christian faith and the how of Christian discipleship, but both are to be seen and interpreted against the background of the Who (the news!) of Jesus Christ. Think about it this way: When a jeweler is going to set a precious stone, the craftsmanship will be totally devoted to casting light properly on the stone at the center of the setting. Precious metals—silver, gold, and platinum—will be chiseled and shaped and polished to reflect the light to give depth to the precious stone. And a variety of semiprecious stones will be cut and turned so that they will refract the maximum amount of light and illumine the centerpiece. An artistic setting is one that attracts attention to and enhances the beauty of the precious stone at the center of it all. I believe the writers of the New Testament were like fine jewelers. Their ultimate concern was for us to see the Hope diamond (or the pearl of great price, if you prefer)

in all its glorious splendor. Our preaching must take a clue from them: The precious metals and semiprecious stones of the New Testament witness reflect and refract the light so that we see clearly Jesus Christ. We must trust those texts and use them in our preaching in the way they were intended: to cast a bright beam of light on the one who is risen from the dead.

Mary Catherine Hilkert, a fine Roman Catholic scholar, has recently written a book that I value as one of the strongest expositions of "homiletical theology" in recent years. The book is overflowing with sound theology for preachers in liturgical traditions. Almost everything in the book would be a great starting place for further development and discussion. Let me take just one of her ideas and work with it here to give you a taste of the riches that are in store for you when you tackle her work.[2] In a discussion of the power of human words, Hilkert notes that human words essentially accomplish two things: They carry information and they have the capacity to create immediate change with lasting results. Words that convey information are important to the daily transactions of human community but do not necessarily carry with them large amounts of raw power. For example, "The closing banquet for the preaching conference will be held this evening in the Hoffman Refectory on Chelsea Square." That's important information for participants in the preaching conference because it tells them when and where they will get something to eat, but it is hardly life-changing information.

On the other hand, words with power to effect change will do two things. They will open up the future or close it down. Take a few examples. Imagine yourself in the "ritual dance" of getting to know another person. You notice each other across the room, meet at the punch bowl, flirt, exchange phone numbers, and go your separate ways. A few days later you meet to have lunch, take in a movie, or go for a stroll in the park. The time together was pleasant and later in the week the two of you get together for dinner and the opera, followed by a nightcap at your favorite tavern. You get the picture. It is the way human beings "dance" their way into relationship with each other, moments filled with anticipation and delight. Then the moment comes. One of you, perhaps with a tight throat and sweaty palms, says, "I love you." Hmm. Power. These are powerful words with the capacity to change the relationship forever. If the hearer of those words is receptive, the future of the relationship may be opened up and deeper romance and relationship may be an immediate and lasting consequence. On the other hand, if the hearer is less receptive, the power of the words "I love you" may frighten and disturb and cause one's friend to flee. Consider another example. A person has been ill for some time. Invasive surgery, radiation, and chemotherapy have been the order of the day. Placing significant hope in the results of the medical treatments, the patient anticipates a slow, but steady recovery. The doctor then enters the room and says, "I'm very sorry, but there is nothing else we can do." Those words carry extremely raw power. The change is immediate and has lasting results.

Think for a moment about the implications of this for preaching the Gospel. If, in addition to carrying information, words have the capacity to open up or close down the future—and in preaching let's consider that to be one's future in God—it is not hard to see how much power is at the preacher's disposal. (What an incredible stewardship. And what potential for abuse!) Ponder with me a sermon on forgiveness. The sermon may carry a large amount of information: biblical teaching on forgiveness, theological ideas that show how forgiveness is related to faith and grace, and perhaps some sacramental theology about confession and reconciliation. The point is, this sermon could be overflowing with information. That's fine and that's good. But given the power at the preacher's disposal to open up the future, the preacher must move beyond the information, as important as it is, and declare God's forgiveness. An informational sermon might conclude: "Given all of the texts we have examined in the last fifteen minutes, it seems reasonable to conclude that God wants to forgive us." A more powerful sermon (with the capacity to effect immediate and lasting change) might conclude: "Friends, the Good News of the Gospel is this: In the Name of Jesus you are forgiven." I am obviously caricaturing this slightly to make the point. We can talk about forgiveness or we can declare forgiveness. They are not mutually exclusive ideas, but it is the declaration of forgiveness that carries the power to change lives.

At this stage I want to return for a few moments to the idea of news and I want to make a bold assertion: People are changed not when words are spoken, but when they are heard. This is not a new idea—plenty of folks have called our attention to it—but it is a profound idea for the preacher to embrace. Allow me to raise the stakes. Consider this statement: The Resurrection of Jesus Christ from the dead never changed anyone's life! Whoa! But think about it. Who was there? No one, basically. There was that angel-guy sitting on the rolled-away stone, but remember, angels are messengers; he heard it from someone else. So Mary and the other women make their way to the tomb. They lug their jars of embalming ointments, fresh cloth to wrap the body of Jesus, perhaps some incense to cover the odor of decaying flesh, and their prayer books. They make their way in the light darkness of early morning, overcome with sadness and despair, and filled with fear at the thought of everything that their future might hold. (Jesus by this time has already been risen for an hour or so and is on his way to the Galilee to surprise the other disciples.) Nothing about the resurrection of the Savior has changed anything in the lives of the women on their way to the tomb. Why? ("Why do you seek the living among the dead?") Because they have not heard. ("He is not here. He is risen!") News! Immediately their lives are changed because they have heard the news that Jesus is risen. And all the while, the other disciples are locked behind closed doors, and as far as they are concerned life is about as desperate as it gets. (Jesus is risen, remember, but they don't know it.) So the women go in haste to the place where the disciples are in mourning with the news that Jesus is risen from the dead. And that news has spread from behind those closed doors to the ends of the earth.

Let's bring this point a little closer home. Several months ago, a dear friend of mine was killed in an automobile accident. At the time of his death, I was frolicking on the Outer Banks of North Carolina with my family completely oblivious to the tragedy. I felt no pain, no sadness, no grief. The rites of Christian burial came and went without my knowledge or participation. His death had no impact upon me. No impact, that is, until last week. Last week, quite by accident, I heard the news of his death. I was shocked, distraught, and in enormous pain. By now many others of our friends were well on their way to healing and relief, but for me his death was as raw as if it had been yesterday. My friend's death caused me no pain, but the news of it almost killed me.

And that, friends, is why we preach. Nothing is more powerful than words that carry news—not information alone, but news that changes our perspectives, reorients our lives, and never leaves us alone. What greater joy could there be than being the mouthpiece of news about God? "Christianity is a Word and someone has to stick it in your ear!" News!

The Reverend Canon J. Neil Alexander, Th.D., is Professor of Homiletics in the School of Theology of the University of the South, Sewanee, Tennessee.

NOTES

1. See the discussion of this idea in Herman G. Stuempfle, *Preaching Law and Gospel* (Philadelphia: Fortress, 1978), 17.

2. Mary Catherine Hilkert, *Naming Grace: Preaching and the Sacramental Imagination* (New York: Continuum, 1997), 58–59.

Tell It Again, Please; Tell It Again!

Jane Sigloh

Now in the days of Samuel the glory of the Lord departed from Israel. The Philistines had captured the ark of the covenant and taken it to the temple in Ashdod. There they put it on a pedestal that was a little lower than the pedestal for their god Dagon.

Early the next morning the women of Ashdod went to the temple and they discovered that the statue of Dagon had fallen off its pedestal—on its face! Its head was shattered in pieces. The hands were broken off and tossed across the threshold. "Dagon has lost his power," they cried, "for he is without a head for thinking and without hands for acting." And all the Philistines trembled. Was this ordinary vandalism or was the hand of the Lord upon them?

They remembered what happened to the Egyptians when they tried to hold back the glory of the Lord. "Maybe we should send the ark of the covenant to the people in Gath," they said. "They have a very nice temple over there. Small, but nice." And so they did, but the people in Gath were suddenly afflicted with plagues, just like the Egyptians. Was the hand of the Lord upon them? The people of Gath took the ark to their neighbors in Ekron. But their neighbors in Ekron were also afflicted with plagues.

Something had to be done! The Philistine elders called for a council. They gathered in a circle under the acacia trees. And talked about the strange power of the ark of the covenant of the Lord. They did a SWOT analysis of their situation. They scrutinized and prioritized and reorganized. Until the grass under their feet began to go to sleep.

Then, when they were about the business of putting their goals and objectives on newsprint, an old woman at the edge of the circle stood up. She was so thin you could sweep her away with a broom. Her arms were blotched and shriveled. Her dress hung like a tent over her body. But the old woman's eyes were like the blue of fire.

She looked around the circle and then she spoke. "The glory of the Lord is in our midst," she said. "It is a presence that is more than a presence. I have heard that heaven is its throne and earth is its footstool. But I tell you it is the force of life. It transforms. It restores. It liberates. You men from Mars think you have captured it and can use it to win your battles and force your agendas. You put it in the temple in

Ashdod. You haul it over to Gath. And then you haul it over to Ekron. You boast, you tremble, you talk and talk and talk. But you don't understand.

"The glory of the Lord has chosen to come into our midst. It has chosen weakness and humiliation. And you had better watch out. Because there is more power, more sovereign splendor in its weakness and humiliation than ever was in the temple of Dagon. Let the ark of the covenant go home." And then the old woman eased her way back to the edge of the circle.

The grass began to move again. The elders mumbled something about old women who talk too much, who stand closer to the soil than the sky. They went back to their goals and objectives. And finally they reached a conclusion. "We must let the ark of the covenant go home."

The decision was made and the Philistines built a new cart for the ark—out of sweet scented algum wood. They laid the ark upon it. And next to it they laid their guilt offerings, images of gold to turn away the hand of the Lord. They found two cows that had never been yoked to pull the cart. And they said "Shoo...cows...git gone!"

And slowly the cows turned their heads to Beth-shemesh! There was no driver! There was no one to lead them, but the cows went neither to the left or to the right, even when they heard the lowing of their newborn calves. They went straight to Beth-shemesh. Every valley was lifted up for them. Every hill was made low. The uneven ground was leveled. And the restless glory of the Lord returned to Israel.

There was great rejoicing in the countryside of Beth-shemesh. The Spirit raised its wild song of praise. "Hoopla! The glory of the Lord has returned." Everyone in the village sang and danced and talked about their self-starting God and how the ark had rolled across the wheat fields—all by itself—with the stone tablets rumbling in the cargo. And when the children heard the part about the statue of Dagon falling on its face, they laughed and laughed, and said "Tell it again!"

And so they did. They didn't explain it, of course. They just told it, because they really didn't understand how God could topple the empty idols of their culture without any help from them. Indeed they didn't understand why God would enter alien land in the first place... and submit to such weakness and humiliation.

So they just told the story. Generation after generation they told it, with a few stretchers here and there...just for effect. And hearing it, people began to believe that there was some overriding purpose for them in history. It was God's purpose and it would prevail. It would prevail.

Over the years more stories were told about the glory of the Lord. People would step out from the edge of the circle and speak. Sometimes with a fiery tongue and sometimes with a gentle whisper. They told sad stories—about how their own people presumed on the freedom of the Lord. They told stories of great wonder—how in a sudden moment of time the axis of the earth...would shift.

How once in the early morning another group of women went to a tomb. They didn't find Dagon with his head shattered in pieces. They found two men in dazzling clothes and the men said, "Why do you look for the living among the dead? He is not here. He is risen." And the axis of the earth...shifted.

"Tell us that story again," they would say, especially when they saw how disease and poverty had eroded the human spirit, especially when they touched the blood of crossfire bullets, especially when they heard Rachael weeping for her children. "Tell us that story again. Tell us how the dark crown of thorns blazed with love."

And someone would step out from the edge of the circle and speak. The uneven ground would be leveled. And the glory of the Lord would spread like wings over their fields. The Spirit would raise its wild song of praise. And the children would say, "Tell it again. Please, tell it again."

Jane Sigloh is rector of Emmanuel Church in Staunton, Virginia.

Section II: Tuning the Senses, Shaping the Resonance

Time out, again. For two concerns, actually.

Concern Number One: How is all this preaching talk affected by the fact that it is taking place "in house"? Preachers preaching to other preachers. Preachers talking to preachers about their preaching.

This preaching conference was initially convened within the confines of a seminary "close"—a little green park, completely quadrangled off from megacity stress and squalor by a bulwark of cloistering buildings. Is there not, perhaps, a bit of irony in that? Is homiletics only "in-house" language uttered by and for an "in group" of theological elites?

Response to Concern One: Point well taken. It is high time, not to shut down the professional conversation, but to broaden it. Time to include preaching that takes place, if not in "the real world" (what world, after all, is "unreal"?), then at least in the context of a wider world. Hence, our homiletical discussions will now be enhanced by sermon speech that was first shaped for faith communities which are not primarily communities of homiletical discernment.

Along with other conference preaching, we will hear sermons that come from north and south, east and west; by preachers who are Black, Hispanic, and Caucasian; who preach in parishes large and small, suburban and rural; on festive occasions and ordinary occasions; in situations ranging from Stewardship Sunday to the last Sunday in a long-term, rector-parish relationship that has not always been smooth. We will hear of deep moral tragedy, and discouraging moral temptation. We will encounter old women and young men, hamsters and dogs, a rabbit and a ferret, all kinds of smells and the sight of blood, a bean taco and a "Tickle Me Elmo" doll.

Perhaps this promise is enough to make us stay tuned. But then there is Concern Number Two—which, to be candid, involves the practical implications of another homiletical "in-house" issue. (Maybe our concern for a wider preaching world was legitimate, but our fears about homiletical "shop talk" were not altogether necessary.)

Concern Number Two: Throughout our discussions thus far, there have been references to "images," "stories," and "ideas." The book itself, in fact, features these words in its title. Why? What exactly is the relevance of image, story, and idea to the vocational ideal of preaching sermons that work?

Response to Concern Number Two: There is nothing technical about these terms, obviously—and, at first glance, nothing obviously important. Of course preachers rely on images, stories, and ideas as they go about trying to "discern patterns of sacred presence" and to "make connections with raw human reality." What else do they have to work with? What else is there for them to work on? Experience is an ever unfolding interplay of

> sensory impressions
> interpersonal interactions, and
> conceptual interpretations.

Our language conveys these distinctive, but interwoven elements through

> images (that paint mental pictures)
> stories (that portray characters in conflict), and
> ideas (that propose analytical insight, based on evidence and argument).

Like other writers and speakers, preachers are word composers. Word composers try to listen for each of these experiential dimensions and language elements. Then they try, in their writing and speaking, to orchestrate all of these authentically and artistically. Preachers, therefore, should not find it surprising that the biblical texts, which serve as fundamental wellsprings of their sacred artistry, are themselves full of images, of stories, and of ideas that are set forth in expository arguments. As in all human language and experience, there is a constant interplay of image, story, and idea within biblical texts. And yet, some biblical texts are much more centered in one form of experience (and one use of language) than others. Paul is forever arguing ideas (even though he employs images and stories in the process). There are arguments and stories implied in the language of the Psalms; but it is images, word pictures, that are primarily employed. The Old Testament chroniclers and the writers of the Gospels use a story form as their stock-in-trade, incorporating imagery and ideas, as appropriate, in the orchestration of their verbal scores.

This, too, is hardly surprising. The literary genres of poetry, narrative, and expository argument are not arbitrary categories. These genres are natural expressions of the different (yet not unrelated) ways in which human beings "make sense" of their experience.

A fragrant, deep red rose "makes sense" in a way rather different than does an eleventh-hour reconciliation between two lovers who have understandably, yet all but tragically, misunderstood each other for years. And the "sense" of each of these is not the same as the "sense" a scientist has when the evidence "all adds up" in light of a new theoretical paradigm.

Poetry is centered in image language. Narratives (novels, dramas, documentaries, etc.) are centered in story language. Expository prose and persuasive oratory are centered in idea, or argument language. The language form that word composers select depends upon their particular artistic bent, and on the particular kind of "sense" they are attempting primarily to capture, and convey.

There is a homiletical word in all of this. Preachers are not likely to be able to "discern the pattern of divine presence," and "make the connection with raw human reality" unless they are on intimate, experiential terms with the related but distinctive language worlds of image, story, and idea. If their knowledge of these is merely "knowledge about," rather than "deep acquaintance with," the only sermons they will probably preach are ones which (as the prologue says) "declare the timeless principle," and "apply it to the sinful situation."

It is no accident that the homiletical lectures we encountered at the Preaching Excellence Conference in Part One had the feel of being uttered by theological musicologists who were themselves deeply sensitive to the music of God's saving word. It was not mere coincidence that the sermons we heard in conjunction with those lectures had the feel of inspiring religious music. All of these players are alert to ways in which sermons that work strike chords, create resonance, move hearts, and give spiritual phrasing and cadence to the ebb and flow of raw human life. Not only can these preachers "discern the patterns" and "make the connections." They are able through their intimate awareness of image, story, and idea to "tune their preaching senses to the mutual singing" of patterns and connections in divine presence and in raw human reality.

It is not enough, however, for preachers to be sensitive to image, story, and idea as these sound forth and sing out to each other in biblical texts and in human dramas. Preachers must also be able (again from the prologue) to "shape sermons that resonate with this music." This involves more than being able to recognize the dynamics of image, story, and idea when one hears and sees them. It involves more than being able to import images, include stories, and inject ideas. Rather, it involves being able to shape whole sermons in accordance with the distinctive timbres and interplaying tonalities of each distinctive mode of experience and language.

Perhaps a direct analogy with the world of literal music will be helpful here. Music is made up of notes, as sermons are made up of words. But notes sound differently when they are played by stringed instruments, by woodwinds, and by instruments that make up the brass choir of an orchestra. (Similarly, the same words will sound very different when, in sermons, they are played as images, as parts of stories, or as arguments for important ideas.)

In a musical concerto, one will hear strings, woodwinds, and brass instruments, just as elements of image, story, and idea/argument language will be heard in interplay throughout any sermon that is well tuned to the mutual singing of sacred pattern and human connection.

In a musical concerto, however, an instrument from one of these choirs will be featured, and "take the lead." If the full orchestra is always playing, we will never be able to recognize what we are hearing as a concerto for clarinet (or for viola, or French horn). In a concerto, all the instruments are engaged, but one predominates. And the instrument that leads makes a decided difference in how the melody sounds, and how the harmony is experienced.

In sermons that work, the particular kind of spiritual resonance achieved is in large measure determined by the predominantly shaping rhetorical form. While images, stories, and ideas are all necessary in order for a sermon to resonate deeply with the strings of the heart, the overtones, as it were, will be scrambled and distorted if the "lead" in the sermon is not taken by one of these three.

All three rhetorical dimensions must be present in a sermon that works, but the shape of the sermon needs to be primarily that of an image, a story, or an argument. This guiding principle is no more a constriction on preaching than its analogue is on orchestrating a concerto. In both cases, the form makes possible freedom in the act of composition, and resonating power in the creative result.

In the following three sections, we will hear fifteen sermon concertos. An equal number are shaped primarily by images projected, by stories told, and by ideas argued (not ideas advocated argumentatively). We will probably be able to recognize easily the shaping influence of the primary rhetorical instrument (and the presence of the supporting instruments as well). We will also be able to discern the marked difference in compositional styles between different sermon composers who are working in the same basic rhetorical idiom.

In some cases, the primary instrument is used with slight, deft touches here and there. In other sermons, the rhetorical strategy is markedly obvious throughout. The stories told will be of quite different kinds. The ideas will be argued with strategies as idiosyncratic as the personalities of the preachers are unique. The ways in which the image sermons strike our senses will probably range from gossamer-light to all-but-overpowering.

Do all these sermons have anything in common? Yes. They are all missing something. Two things, actually. Not a one of them (to return once again to the prologue) simply "finds a 'hook' to grab attention." None of them struggles and strains to "serve up truths that are 'interesting' and 'relevant.' " Which is to say, of course, that these sermons, too, are sermons that sing, sermons that work.

Preaching in Image Form

Going Home

Michael Goldberg

❧

There is probably no stronger urge for a human being than the sense of "home." That place where you are known, and you know. That place where you can say, "I was born there..." or "I belong..." or "I started there."

"Home" is that place where you can relax, and truly be yourself. It is a safe place, an area where there is no pretense.

Ezra and Paul are interested in home as well: Ezra as he deals with the reconstruction of the Second Temple in Jerusalem; Paul as he writes a second, or maybe even a third letter to the Corinthians, a troubled Christian community in Greece.

The focus of Israel's religion was in the Temple. The Temple was where God's presence, his Spirit, would dwell. The daily sacrifices, the rituals, the prayers, the rabbinical scholars conducting their individual yeshivas were all under the umbrella of the House of the Lord. All this had been taken away when Babylon had conquered Judah—destroying Israel's religious life, her nationhood, and the Temple as well.

With Persia's conquering of Babylon, the people of Israel were finally permitted to go home and rebuild their sacred space. The exiles were finally coming home—but this "home" was a place of desolation and defeat. It takes the foresight of Ezra and Nehemiah to rally the people and to remind them of just who has brought them out of slavery and into the new life of grace.

Paul of Tarsus, too, has to remind the people of the Church in Corinth that it is the Lord Jesus Christ who has brought the gift of new life and hope to the Gentile community in the city. He writes:

> *And I hope that, although you do not know us very well yet, you will have come to recognize, when the day of our Lord Jesus comes, that you can be as proud of us as we are of you.* 2 Corinthians 1:14 (JB)

The sense of home and roots in the power of God, through Jesus Christ, was the mainstay for Paul in all his missionary journeys. It gave him the strong sense of authority for him to proclaim, not in his own name, but in the name of the Risen One, who called him to apostleship on the road to Damascus.

The blessing of home was brought home to me more powerfully when a gentleman, who had been attending my parish in Trenton, came up in the middle of Lent and said quite plainly, "I wish to be a follower of Jesus!"

Here I was, the rector of a parish in the midst of a busy Lenten season, presented with the opportunity to celebrate the first catechumenate process in my work; and I just knew that I couldn't do the whole three-year procedure in only three weeks! I called a priest in a neighboring parish and asked him, "What is the best way to handle this pastoral situation?" He said simply, "The man has requested to be a follower of Jesus. What more catechesis do you need?"

I took the sage advice and proceeded to instruct Peter about baptism and his entrance into the Christian community. His wife and children were already members of the church. In point of fact, Lucille, Peter's wife, had told her husband that he could become a member of the Christian Church *only* if he was baptized at the Great Vigil of Easter, just as she had been so many years before. She wants them all to worship together. Then their home would be a "Christian home."

The night of the Great Vigil arrived. The clergy in the Trenton area gather with the bishop at the cathedral, to celebrate the Easter Moment together. Baptisms, confirmations, and receptions were all part of the witness of the Easter Even congregation. On this night of nights, Peter was the sole candidate for baptism. When the bishop asked him if his intention was to be baptized, Peter replied, "I do." He had memorized the whole baptismal rite. As he approached the waters of the font, he very intentionally took upon himself the life of the resurrected Christ.

There wasn't a dry eye in the place. Peter's act of faith, his earnestness, and humility caused us all to pause and re-collect why this sacrament is a model for wholeness and community. Peter was welcomed home. He was welcomed by his bishop at the peace. He was welcomed by his wife as they made communion together for the first time. He was welcomed as Christ's own forever as he was marked with the oils and christened. Peter had now arrived at his destination, as "being a follower of Jesus."

Trying to establish his credentials with the hostile Corinthian community, Paul pleaded:

Remember it is God himself who assures us all, and you, of our standing in Christ and has anointed us, marking us with his seal and giving us the pledge, the Spirit, that we carry in our hearts. 2 Corinthians 1:21–22 (JB)

We all strive for homecoming as we search for completeness in our lives. At times, we think that we can do it simply on our own. We can't help it; after all we are Americans, and we are taught that the rugged individualist is more to be admired than one who seeks to form community.

And yet, in both of our readings, we are given a glimpse of that sense of wholeness and felicity which comes from those who continue to keep alive the apostles' teaching and fellowship, who break the bread of unity and offer prayers for those within and without the community. In our striving to find completeness, we are found by God. And in being found by God, we are given that sense of being "home." That place where we have a place and identity. And for that gift of grace, we join our spirit with those who pray through the Lord Jesus Christ and say, "Amen, Amen."

Michael Goldberg is rector of St. Augustine's Episcopal Church in Vero Beach, Florida.

Your Presence Is Requested—Wedding Garment Required

Penelope Duckworth
Isaiah 25: 1–9; Psalm 23; Philippians 4:4–13; Matthew 22:1–14

Last month I was in southern Ohio helping my father clear out my grandfather's house. In an upstairs room was a large trunk full of very old clothes. There were boned and bustled dresses from the mid-nineteenth century, unbleached muslin infant gowns, umbrellas with wooden skeletons, narrow black ankle boots, beaver hats. Few had any indication of the owner but two had faded papers pinned to them. One was a man's brown velvet vest. My great grandmother had carefully penned and attached the label "grandpa's wedding vest."

Many families preserve wedding garments. I remember as a child the magic of seeing my mother's wedding veil attached to waxlike flowers in a drawer at my grandmother's house. I have boxed and saved my own wedding gown, and my nine-year-old daughter keeps beseeching me to take it down from the closet shelf. Weddings are important. The clothes worn have significance; and not just the clothes of bride and groom. Those who attend wear appropriate attire to honor the parties and the occasion. This is a premise in the Gospel story we hear today.

Upon first reading, however, we may be dismayed at the king's behavior. We could easily conclude that the king in the parable behaves like the etiquette police. He is angered by the guests who refuse to respond to his invitation. When those who do respond come inappropriately dressed, he casts them into the outer darkness. He seems harsh and unfair. But let's stay with the parable and reflect on its meaning.

A parable is a story that works like a metaphor. It tells us something, but it is also telling us about something else. The Gospel story Jesus tells points us toward another story. That story is our own story, the story of our life in relation to God. God invites us to a great feast, a marriage feast which is deeper communion with the divine, with God, and others. But most of us postpone responding. We would like a little more time in the world. We would like to have a shot at making our own way on our own terms. We will hold off a relationship with God until we're older when "those issues" become more insistent.

But things change. God does not just wait idly by, and neither do we. We change, and are changed, by the way in which we spend our days. And something in us atrophies when we postpone and refuse the invitation. Some things in our lives will not come to fruition. We will not learn some lessons; and we will be the poorer for it.

Others are called to the feast and go. We see it as we grow older. Sometimes the least-expected people go on to become wise and wonderful human beings. We see them ennobled by suffering, and showing a largesse of spirit that astounds us. Likewise, we see people who showed great promise being diminished and even deformed by the directions their lives have taken.

Clearly some have gone to the feast and flourished there, and others turned their backs on the invitation. However, occasionally there is someone who goes to the feast but has left some aspect of her- or himself poorly prepared; and the lack of preparation becomes evident. Perhaps he cannot cope with success or power, and misuses it. Or she may have only done part of the authentic work on herself that the invitation presumed and encouraged. He might be loving to many, but cruel to those close to him. Such ones are not properly prepared or attired for the feast.

Yet what does it mean to be properly attired and how do we become that way? A poem by the Anglican priest and poet George Herbert may help. He begins:

> *Prayer is the Church's banquet, Angels' age,*
> *God's breath in man returning to his birth,*
> *The soul in paraphrase, heart in pilgrimage,*
> *The Christian plummet sounding heav'n and earth...*

In the third stanza he describes prayer as

> *Softness, and peace, and joy, and love, and bliss*
> *Exalted Manna, gladness of the best,*
> *Heaven in ordinary, man well drest...*[1]

Herbert tells us that prayer and "man well drest" are related. A well-dressed person is one who is prepared for life and what life brings. Prayer enables one to become that way. We all know the feeling of being fully ready for an event. A wedding is a case in point. Great amounts of time and expertise go into the preparation of bride and groom. When we have all the necessary preparation done, and we feel complete and ready for what is to come, then we are well-dressed.

Herbert is speaking of spiritual readiness and completion. In prayer our essential selves are in touch with the presence of God and suffused with the love of God. Another dimension has been added to our being. You recall how Moses' face shone after he met with the living God on Mount Sinai. And remember how Jesus' clothes became white beyond the capacity of any bleach on the mountain of the Transfiguration. Conversation with God clothes us with a new layer through which we filter reality. We become dressed with the grace of God.

Teresa of Avila once wrote to her nuns, "Would it not be a sign of great ignorance, my daughters, if a person were asked who he was, and could not say and had no idea who his father or his mother was, or from what country he came? Though that is great stupidity, our own is incomparably greater if we make no attempt to discover what we are, and only know that we are living in these bodies, and have a vague idea because we have heard it and because our Faith tells us so, that we possess souls. As to what good qualities there may be in our souls, or Who dwells within them or how precious they are—those are things which we seldom consider...."[2]

Today's Gospel parable is about the wedding feast of the soul with God. Jesus, like Teresa after him, is pointing out that there is a spiritual reality that is usually ignored. Most people are too busy to come to the wedding. But that doesn't mean that the wedding doesn't happen or that, for better or for worse, the soul's life doesn't go on.

Matthew addressed his Gospel to the Jews and he emphasized the teachings of Jesus that spoke directly to Jewish Christians. This parable tells the Jewish Christians that although they are the chosen people of God, their recalcitrance will render them replaceable. It was a warning to them not to rest on their laurels, their preferred position with God. The same can be said of any of us, even Episcopalians, who have sometimes been described as elevating good taste to an article of faith. Our task is to be continually well-dressed in the deeper sense.

But this parable seems to be asking more of us than to keep open communication with God. It asks a readiness of us. Procrastination can be a spiritual as well as a temporal hazard. Jesus teaches us that much of being well-dressed spiritually is being ready to respond to what life offers. Let me give you an example: I found the following letter in the newspaper, in Ann Landers's column, several years ago.

"Dear Ann—I feel I must reply to the man who wrote to say that he couldn't love an adopted child as much as his own, therefore he would rather not have any children.

"Katie was the most popular girl on campus. I was called the Brain.... One afternoon, I came across Katie crying her heart out on a bench behind the library. We were good friends, and she told me she was pregnant. I offered to marry her then and there and she accepted. A minister performed the ceremony the following weekend. It was June and we both graduated ten days later. I had an offer to go to South America which I accepted. We left together as Mr. and Mrs.

"That was fourteen years ago, Ann. Our firstborn son has a brother and two sisters. But he is the child dearest to my heart.—No Signature, of Course."[3]

The author of that letter was prepared. He was prepared for what life would give him. He was literally ready with his wedding garment. And he proved his readiness not only in his enduring relationship with his wife but likewise with the child she was carrying.

Mark Doty, in his recent memoir, *Heaven's Coast*, writes, "What I have come to love about being an adult, to the extent that I can claim that title, [is] that one knows more about how good things are, how much they matter, as they are happening; that knowledge isn't necessarily retrospective anymore." He continues, "When I was younger, I missed so much, failing to be fully present, only recognizing the quality of particular moments and gifts after the fact. Perhaps that's one thing that being "grown-up" is: to realize in the present the magnitude or grace of what we're being offered."[4]

This Gospel story is one that tells of grace happening now; and it urges us to move into the maturity of our calling. I am reminded of those many scripture readings that we usually hear in Advent, but which are applicable at all times. We are warned to be ready, to be prepared, because we do not know when Christ will come again. We are called to respond to the invitation now. We do not know how much time we have. We do not know which day will be our last. We do not know when everything will be required of us; so our task is to be in right relationship with God now.

Be prepared. Have that wedding garment washed, pressed, and hanging ready to be slipped into at a moment's notice. The invitation could be in the mail as I speak. That sound in the distance could be Mendelssohn's wedding march. The honor of your presence is requested.

Penelope Duckworth serves the Stanford Canterbury Foundation in Stanford, California.

NOTES

1. George Herbert, *The Selected Poems of George Herbert,* edited by Joseph H. Summers, (New York: Signet, 1967), 90.

2. Teresa of Avila, *Interior Castle*, translated by E. Allison Peers (Garden City, N.Y.: Doubleday, 1961), 29.

3. Permission is granted by Ann Landers, Creators Syndicate.

4. Mark Doty, *Heaven's Coast* (New York: Harper Collins, 1996), 90.

God Is a Knitter

Sara Scott Wingo

My grandmother was a knitter. In her lifetime she knit many beautiful sweaters, scarves, and blankets.

She was born in 1904, the second daughter of Eliza Lowrie Hamilton, who was a redhead, and Harry Scott Grayson in Washington, Pennsylvania, near Pittsburgh. They named her Sara Scott after her grandmother Grayson, but during her childhood they called her Sally. Once when she was away at boarding school, Sara Scott playfully told a roommate who was on her way out one night that she looked like Medusa. The roommate responded that she would think up a horrible name for Sara Scott and make it stick. My grandmother was called Sadie from that day forth. This playful good humor characterized all her days.

But I digress. My grandmother was a knitter. She was fond of taking beautiful yarns, ones with soft, fuzzy textures and brilliant multicolors, and knitting scarves for her friends. She also made sweaters for her grandchildren and great-grandchildren and many blankets. These objects were the prize of all who were so lucky as to be gifted with them.

There is a picture of my grandmother as a young child of about five years old. She is sitting with her legs crossed at the ankle, and there is a perfectly impish grin upon her face, a grin that seems to be an invitation to come and play. One feels an impulse to take her up on the invitation and to jump into the picture and join her; but being bound by time and space such a thing is not possible. My family has often marveled that my daughter, Graycie, closely resembles the little girl in the picture. It almost seems as if they could be twin sisters.

When I was a little girl, my grandmother taught me to knit. It took a while to get the hang of it, but before long I too was knitting socks and blankets. I learned very quickly the pleasure of thinking about the person for whom you are making a gift during the long, quiet hours of work and the anticipation of the joy of gift-giving.

My grandmother died at the end of January this year, and my second daughter, Anna, was born a month later. She is a redhead. My grandmother had made her a blanket. It was the last one she ever knitted. It is yellow and has a beautiful, wavelike pattern knit in it. By the time my grandmother had made it, she was blind. At one point, she lost the flow of the pattern, and reversed it. The reversed pattern flows to the end of the blanket.

When Anna was very young and when I had finally gotten her to sleep and tucked under her yellow blanket, I would stand and stare at her, awestruck by the miracle of her life, and of my love for her. I knew that this love was powerful enough to cover her all the days of her life, and flawed though it might be, I prayed that it would be pure enough to give her strength and add joy to her living. I had the sense that the love I experienced in that moment did not originate in me, but that it came to me from the many previous generations of parents who had loved their children. There was also the sense that the love came from God.

Anna turns out to be the spitting image of another great-grandmother. She looks like her daddy, who looks like his daddy, who looks like his mother, who was a redhead. Her name too was Sara, and when my husband was a little boy, she and he adored each other. I had not known my husband for more than a day when I began to hear of this beloved grandmother who had died years ago. I'm not really sure why my husband fell in love with me so quickly, but my name could not have hurt. I am glad. When he asked me to marry him, he gave me her ring. Years later I gave birth to a child who looks like she could have been her twin sister. Sara Wingo and I lived in different times and different places, but surely our lives are intertwined.

So it is with all of us. All of our lives are intertwined with one another and with all the saints who have gone before. The gift of the saints to us is not so much the perfection of their love, for they were flawed human beings like the rest of us; their gift rather is the power of their love that flows from God, through them, to us. This love unites us to them, and adds strength and joy to our lives. The communion of all the saints points us to the reality that God is a knitter. The one of whom the psalmist said, "You knit me together in my mother's womb," is the same one to whom we pray this morning saying, "You have knit together your elect in one communion and fellowship in the mystical body of your Son Christ our Lord."

We are tied to one another in the bonds of God's love, tied so closely that the boundaries of time and space begin to fall away; and we find that even those who lived in ages past are our companions today. I think of Francis of Assisi who renounced the luxury of wealth to find the true riches of God, of how the simple beauty of nature and all its creatures filled his heart with joy. I think of Julian of Norwich who lived during a time of great tumult. The Black Plague struck down many in her day, and the Church was in desperate need of reform. Yet the peace of God filled her, and made her able to say and believe, "All will be well and all will be well." I think of Martin, a Southerner of our own century, an outcast because of the color of his skin, who spoke so eloquently of the brotherhood and sisterhood of us all that he led a once slave-trading nation to examine what it means to respect the dignity of every human being. I think of my grandmother, of my husband's grandmother, and other grandparents. I think of my family and friends, and I think of you all who in this time and place seek to be a family to each other, all of them and all of you, brothers and sisters in Christ, and companions in the way.

My grandmother died in the middle of the night. After we received the phone call, I had a dream as I dozed in and out of sleep. A little girl came and played with me. We ran through grassy meadows and did somersaults and laughed, as if I were a child, too. It came time for us to part, so I held up my hand to the hand of this dream visitor. I saw my own thirty-four-year-old hand and the hand of an aged woman. It was my grandmother's hand, the hand of that great knitter, next to mine. I knew in that moment that death had not diminished her, but through some strange working of God's grace she had been made strong and whole; and I knew then, as I still know now, that her love strengthens me and adds joy to my living. In the dream, the boundaries of time and space fell away. So it is for all of us who are caught up in the mystery of God's love; we are knit together in one great communion where peace and joy abound. We are knit together, even the living with the dead.

"Oh blest communion, fellowship divine! We feebly struggle, they in glory shine; yet all are one in thee, for all are thine, Alleluia, alleluia!"

Sara Scott Wingo serves St. Philip's Church in Birmingham, Alabama.

A Certain Unmistakable Fragrance

Charles Rice

What will you take home with you from this week together?

In this chapel and in the close garden, through many homilies and late conversations, in the refectory and with our roommates, we have tasted and touched, heard and seen many gifts.

Anything olfactory?

How does this place smell? Will we—could we—carry that home with us, to the comfortable summer suburbs or the mean streets?

On another visit to New York, I went to church as I was leaving the city, at St. Mary the Virgin, in the theater district. At the offering I opened my flight bag for my wallet. Back home a few hours later, I unzipped the bag and out came, right there in my bedroom in Madison, New Jersey, a puff of the Holy Eucharist at Smoky Mary's!

You probably have enough of Haggai and Ezra for the trip home, so tuck into your bag a piece of Paul's second letter to his difficult friends in Corinth. We have to read between the lines for what prompts this letter. Let us just say that people, Paul among them, have been hurt and disappointed, unremarkable for people trying to live together, especially in the Church.

Paul says three quite remarkable things.

First, he says that he does not take it personally. Whatever has happened affects the whole community; and whatever resolution comes will be from and for the sake of the whole community: "But if anyone has caused pain, he has caused it not to me, but in some measure...to you all" (2:5).

This is not just a matter of my ego or wounded pride, the sort of thing for which I would carry a grudge or seek recompense. Our life, including our failures and transgressions, is in community, not a matter of private reckoning.

The very idea of the personal, for Paul, includes the community, and is distinguished from the merely private, a distinction important to draw in preaching, by the way. We need more personal, less private, preaching, preaching which is organic to a community's life as embodied in the preacher.

The Apostle goes on to amplify the idea by saying that he forgives for the sake of the community: "What I have forgiven, if I have forgiven anything, has been for your sake in the presence of Christ, to keep Satan from gaining the advantage over us" (2:10–11). Paul forgives for the community's sake, "in the presence of Christ."

Is not this what we see on Sunday morning, when people confess their sins corporately, exchange signs of reconciliation, and come to communion together? This is where Satan is thwarted, where in the presence of Christ and for his sake, people forgive and are forgiven.

And where this happens, Paul concludes, there is a certain unmistakable fragrance: "But thanks be to God, who in Christ always leads us in triumph, and through us spreads the fragrance of the knowledge of him everywhere. For we are the aroma of Christ to God among those who are being saved and among those who are perishing, to one a fragrance from death to death, to the other a fragrance from life to life" (2:14–16).

The life of a gracious community, like each act of forbearance and forgiveness, is like an unmistakable aroma.

Smells are in these days. The sense of smell has the power to bring back significant scenes from our past, and the body responds to healing aromas. Spas now specialize in treatment through smell, and you can easily have aroma therapy in your own bathtub. Someone said recently that if things continue as they are now going, we will go into our well-provided bathrooms in the morning and not emerge until evening!

Health and wholeness through the nose.

St. Paul describes Christians as aromatic, having a fragrance coming from Christ which is pleasing to God.

Christians have a certain smell, like Carl, the world's champion maker of catfish bait. The secret of catfish bait, according to television's interviewer, is that it must smell to "high heaven." Carl's bait does, and so does Carl. He smells like his work, and he doesn't seem to mind that he is not invited to many dinner parties.

That's Paul, this smelling like who we are and what we do:

"We are not...peddlers of God's word; but...we speak in Christ." In short, Paul says that we are what we do. We love our work, and we smell like it!

At a conference, I found my roommate sniffing my sheets. He explained that he was just trying to get to know me!

Each of us does have a distinctive smell—as my two dogs well know.

What would be the fragrance of Christians? What names shall we choose? Boss? Hombre?

If those outside the church were choosing names, what would those be?

The sermons this week have given us a few possibilities:

"Connection," "Glory," or maybe "Angelic"! How about "Charity 490" or "Eau de Decrease"?

There are some pretty good ones on the floor of this beautiful church, what someone called the "yellow brick road" leading to the altar and to the Heavenly City. Look at the words in those little tiles, leading us closer to Christ as we, on the way, absorb and exude his fragrance.

Justice.
  Temperance.
    Mercy.
      Grace.

Do Christians smell like that? Is that the fragrance they get from Christ?

I have smelled this in those little circles of candid charity in which we have tried to listen to each other's homilies, and to learn from one another.

This was unmistakable at a staff meeting late one night. Someone had offended, someone had been hurt, and a spirit of exclusion, even punishment, rose up quite naturally. Then someone spoke—words any one of us could have spoken but had momentarily forgotten—and a certain fragrance spread through the room.

What do Christians smell like, and where do they get this aroma?

You are the aroma of Christ, pleasing to God.

Perhaps some of you have seen the recent issue of the *General Seminary News*, showing a scene in this chapel, just those pews there, under the inscription "...in the Church of God." It is a very peaceful scene; in fact, the eight or ten students and faculty, including the dean, seem at first glance to be asleep! They, of course, are not, sitting there together with their eyes closed in wordless prayer, maybe letting the homily soak in, or just being in the presence of Christ together.

I would like to think that they are savoring something, like someone closing her eyes to smell a rose on one of these June mornings, drinking deeply together of the fragrance of Christ.

What better way to describe our worship, or the life of a seminary, our life in the Church, than stopping to smell the roses, to enter into the grace and peace that is the aroma of Christ.

The picture from which Paul draws these words is a triumphal procession, accompanied by incense, celebrating victory. Christ leads the procession, and the fragrance that spreads along the way is life-giving to all who seek the way. It is in this procession that we walk, the celebration of the Crucified and Risen Savior, whose Gospel we preach.

"How beautiful are the feet of those who preach the Gospel, who tell good news."

These feet are especially beautiful because they have been washed and sent out by Jesus, and because they go forth to preach the Gospel of God's grace and love to all.

Remember the woman who broke open the costly jar and anointed Jesus before his passion and death, and the promise that wherever the Gospel is preached, like the perfume filling the house that day, the memory of her act will be remembered and spread abroad.

The perfume that was poured out that day, which was poured out on the Friday of his death, that is poured out still in his name; that fragrance has a name.

The fragrance of Christ which we bear, in which we live and die, which we preach, thanks be to God, is love.

No doubt you and I will be taking some of that home from these days together and, God willing, catching a whiff of it every time we stand up to preach.

Charles Rice is a priest in the Diocese of Newark and Professor of Homiletics, Drew University.

Martyr's Blood: The Martyrs of Uganda

Linda Clader
Hebrews 10:32–39; Matthew 24:9–14

Collect of the Day: O God, by your providence the blood of the martyrs is the seed of the Church: Grant that we who remember before you the blessed martyrs of Uganda, may, like them, be steadfast in our faith in Jesus Christ, to whom they gave obedience, even to death, and by their sacrifice brought forth a plentiful harvest; through Jesus Christ our Lord, who lives and reigns with you and the Holy Spirit, one God, for ever and ever. Amen.

Did you really pray that prayer with me a few minutes ago?
Did you really say, "Amen"?
Did you listen? Do you know what you prayed for?

A hundred years ago, Anglican and Roman Catholic missionaries brought Christianity into Uganda. They did it with permission from the king, but he would only allow them to preach the Gospel to members of the royal court.

Then that king died, and a new king came into power—a king named Mwanga. Mwanga was not at all happy to discover that the new Christian converts in his own court put their loyalty to Christ above their loyalty to the king. This new king ordered that no one was to go near a Christian mission on pain of death. The converts went anyway, and so Mwanga began an attempt to wipe out Christianity.

On June 3, 1886, he condemned thirty-two young men, pages in his court, to be burned alive. As the young men walked to their deaths, they sang hymns and prayed for their enemies. And the bystanders were so inspired by their witness that they asked the surviving Christians to teach them about Jesus, and Christianity began to spread quickly throughout Uganda.

Faith in Jesus Christ was no longer the foreign religion of white missionaries; now the missionaries to Uganda were Ugandans, and so was the faith. Christianity had been made Ugandan by the shedding of Ugandan blood.

That's what we just prayed about. We prayed to be like those young

Ugandan men, a hundred years ago. We prayed to be steadfast in our faith, like them. And didn't we all say, "Amen"?

But again, just twenty years ago, thousands more Ugandan Christians were slaughtered, under Muslim dictatorship—including the Anglican Archbishop of the Church of Uganda, Janani Luwum. And again, Ugandans and Christians around the world drew inspiration and hope from the witness of these Ugandan martyrs. And that's what we just prayed about.

We prayed to be like Archbishop Luwum, and those martyrs of Uganda. We prayed to be steadfast in our faith, like them. And didn't we all say "Amen"? It's still happening, of course. It's happening all over. Jane Sigloh shared with me the diocesan paper from her diocese, Southwestern Virginia—and in it were story after story about how Christians are being persecuted in their companion diocese in the Church of the Sudan. Over a million Christians have been killed there. But the bishop of this companion diocese says that in the last thirteen years the number of Christian churches in his diocese has gone from 5 to 280. In the last thirteen years, the number of his pastors has gone from 5 to 120 ordained priests. In 1993, this bishop confirmed 10,000 people in a refugee camp.

And the bishop tells a story. He tells of a man of the Sudan, not long ago, who stood in front of a military armored tank, holding his Bible and a cross, and the soldiers killed him and cut him to pieces. And because of that act, says the bishop, 32,000 people "came to the Lord."

We just prayed to be like that man in front of the tank. We just prayed to be like the million dead. By their sacrifice, says the prayer we just prayed, they brought forth a plentiful harvest. That prayer we just prayed says the blood of the martyrs is the seed of the Church. Grant that we may, like them, be steadfast in our faith in Jesus Christ...even unto death. Did you say "Amen"?

We said, "Amen." "Amen," to obedience. "Amen," to steadfast faith. "Amen," to blood.

I have to admit that I'm pretty ambivalent about blood. I hear a story like the one about the man and the tank, and part of me is ready to jump right in there and be a martyr along with him. You know, somebody who does something really big. Somebody who makes a difference. "And because of her courageous act, 32,000 souls came to know the Lord." That sort of thing.

And because I'm a preacher, and a teacher of preachers, of course I translate that kind of impulse of mine into a sort of homiletical mode:

I stand courageously before the world, and proclaim boldly the Good News of Jesus Christ.

Because of my eloquence, because of my impassioned delivery, because of the brilliance of my exegesis, because of the provocative illustrations and stories I come up with, because of how disarmingly authentic I am—I draw thousands to faith in the Gospel. And, like St. Stephen, and St. Paul, and like Martin Luther King and Archbishop Oscar Romero, and like Archbishop Luwum of Uganda, I put a seal on my authenticity as a preacher by making the ultimate sacrifice. A really successful martyr gets to decrease and increase at the same time.

But you know, I really don't want it to hurt very much. For starters, I'd like all that brilliant exegesis and eloquence to come naturally to me—I mean, if it's really a gift, you shouldn't have to work at it, right? And then, if possible, I'd like to be heroic without making anybody mad at me, O.K.? Well, I guess the enemy, whoever they are, could be mad, but not members of my congregation—not my friends—not family members.

The good, Christian people would be on my side, and they'd be cheering. And I'm sure that God would be letting me know in no uncertain terms that I was on the right track, that I had God on my side, at my elbow, supporting my every step.

Having God with me would give me courage, and of course it would also look impressive—it would help lead more people to the faith.

When I get to this point in my fantasy, I find my heart beating just a little faster, in excitement. I wonder how many of us professional Christians have ever harbored our own secret fantasies about martyrdom. And I wonder, when we imagined ourselves in those heroic poses, how much blood we saw on the ground around us. My own secret martyr fantasies never have any blood in them. And I think that's an important clue for me. It's a clue to me that all those martyr fantasies are the wrong kind of thinking. They're the increase kind of thinking, rather than the decrease kind.

Because I think the blood is essential for real martyrdom—not because that's the only way a martyr can die—and not even because we talk about spilling blood when we really mean spilling life. I think the blood part of the martyr picture is essential, because of the messiness factor.

Blood spatters. Blood squirts. Blood is sticky, and when it gets on something, it can be hard to get off. Blood stains things. Carpets, clothes, the ground, cathedral steps. If a martyr or somebody is bleeding a lot, it's not a pretty sight. It doesn't look heroic. You look terrible when you're bleeding to death.

You know, when I imagine that picture of myself as the heroic martyr, my heart runs a little faster with the excitement of the fantasy. But when I think about being sprawled unconscious in a pool of my own blood, I feel only distaste and maybe even embarrassment. I don't get that uplifted feeling. I don't even get an oceanic sort of feeling. In fact, I'm kind of turned off by the whole thing.

I bet those real martyrs in Uganda weren't excited by a vision of their own sacrifice.

I bet the archbishop wasn't. And I bet Jesus wasn't, either.

I don't think the life of a real martyr is a life of heroic visions, or noble feelings.

Being a real martyr, being a witness to the Gospel, is about just putting one foot in front of the other, day after day, and walking step by step in the direction you hear God calling you. It's not an otherworldly, larger-than-life sort of business. It's a flesh-and-blood sort of business. Sticky stuff, messy stuff, even dirty stuff. The kind of stuff you and I live with, and in, and around—every normal day of our lives. The kind of stuff that's run-of-the-mill, and often out of control, and now and then embarrassing. The kind of stuff that, a lot of the time, we want to push out of the way in our attempts to be faithful to the call of Christ.

And then, once in a while, one of us takes all that messy, sticky, embarrassing stuff of life, and shyly, secretly, when no one is looking, lays the whole mess on God's altar—an offering, such as it is.

And that messy, little everyday life is taken, and blessed, and broken and shared with the world. That sort of thing, of course, could happen here.

Linda Clader teaches at the Church Divinity School of the Pacific in Berkeley, California.

PREACHING IN STORY FORM

Be Not Afraid!

Karen B. Johnson
Matthew 28:1–10

༄

Imagine yourself there, as one of those women who have gone to the tomb. It is just before dawn when time hovers uneasily between the dark of night and the light of day. And oh, how dark night has been. These women were surely tear-soaked with grief and staggering with horror. Think for a moment of one you love with all your heart, imagine having watched that precious one publicly stripped, whipped, ridiculed, laid out on bars of wood, nailed to a cross; and then having listened as this beloved one cried out for hours and finally died from lack of breath. This is what those women had lived through. And if they had slept at all in the intervening hours, it must have been that sleep which comes when we are so spent from weeping, that sleep overtakes us just until the body's energy is restored enough to take up again the sobs that feel as if they'll never end.

As Matthew tells the story, two of these women, Mary Magdalene and another, also called Mary, had not only witnessed the gruesome crucifixion, but also, later that night, the burial. Joseph of Arimathea, after securing permission from Pilate, had removed the dead man from the cross, wrapped the corpse in a burial shroud, and carried him to his own tomb where he buried Jesus. The two women had seen all this. And now, hours later, before dawn, they have returned to look at the sepulcher once more.

I know the need they had to look at that sepulcher; and I expect you do, too. One of my seminary classmates died halfway through our senior year. Bob had spent many evenings at our apartment and my children knew him well. He was a jolly fellow, twinkling eyes always looking with affection and merriment from behind his round wire-rimmed glasses. He had been a highly successful businessman turned politician whose heart condition, diagnosed when he turned forty, revolutionized his life. We often heard him make the statement: "This heart condition is the single most positive thing that has ever happened to me." He knew God had not given him the heart condition, but as with all afflictions, that God would not squander it. It had made Bob recognize and pursue his deepest heart's desire: deepening his relationship with, and serving, the living, loving Lord.

While he walked across campus one night, after a party celebrating the end of semester exams, his heart gave out.

Susan, my oldest child, then ten, asked if she could have his glasses. She kept them close at hand for months. We all went frequently to the tree planted in grateful remembrance of him, where his ashes were scattered. Something in these actions, keeping the glasses and visiting the tree, helped. It helped us move beyond the horror and sense of loss at his death, and towards coming to terms with realities we did not want, but knew we had to face. It is essential to mourn our losses if the truths they disclose are to become nourishment for life rather than bitter resentments.

So the two Marys, while shadows of night still covered the earth, went to see the sepulcher. For there were truths there which they, too, desperately wished were otherwise, but knew they had to face. They were certain, of course, about what they would find. The authorities, suspecting Jesus' followers might steal the body and try to convince people he had risen from death, had petitioned Pilate to seal the tomb—making it impossible to roll away the stone—and to set a guard at its entryway. So what the women saw, peering through the pre-dawn darkness, was no surprise. The guards were there, the tomb was sealed shut. The certainty of what had happened hung everywhere.

And just then heaven crashed into the scene. There was a great earthquake as the power of God bolted into the darkness through an angel's descent. The angel, whose appearance was like lightning, rolled back the stone and then sat resolutely upon it. The whole event sent shockwaves through the guards who collapsed in a dead faint. The power of the scene was matched only by its tenderness as the angel spoke to the women. "Be not afraid," he said.

The words ring with familiarity. They are the same as those the angel Gabriel had announced to another frightened Mary, some thirty years earlier, when telling her the news of her scandalous pregnancy. "Be not afraid, the Lord is with you," Gabriel had said. Nine months later another angel had spoken the same words to a group of terrified shepherds out in the countryside watching their flocks by night: "Be not afraid," sounded the heavenly voice, "for behold I bring you good news of a great joy. For to you is born this day in the city of David the Savior who is Christ the Lord."

In the gloom of that dawn at the garden tomb, the angel had a familiar, and yet, as always, stunning announcement: "Be not afraid, for I know that you seek Jesus who was crucified. He is not here, for he has risen." Everything was suddenly turned upside down and inside out. Their certainties were shattered as the astonishing announcement disproved all the presumptions that had brought them to that awful place, and bid them, instead, to believe what was unbelievable.

When we hear the resurrection story, we may be tempted to respond to it as if it is a puzzling problem asking for an intellectual decision. Is it true or not? Perhaps you read the article in this morning's *Washington Post* on the three schools of thought dominating this current debate. I so appreciated the remarks of Luke Johnson, Candler School of Theology Professor of New Testament: "The real experience of the resurrection is the empowering presence of Jesus among his followers after his death. When one focuses on such things as 'Where are the bones?' one has reduced the mystery to a problem. To reduce it to the level of a broken carburetor is to destroy it utterly."

With Luke Johnson I believe the depths of this story's claims go far beyond challenging us to make up our minds whether it's factual. For saying "yes" or "no" to this story means the complete ordering not just of our minds, but also of our lives. After all, if Jesus is raised from the dead, there is absolutely nothing in this world to fear: not the illnesses that befall us, not the brokenness of our relationships, not the loneliness of our lives, not the wounds of our pasts, not the bleakness of our situations, not the sorrows of an eleven-year shepherd/flock union culminating, not the stubbornness of our sin, not the uncertainties of our future, not the radical newness Jesus always summons us to, not even the specter of our own death. With truth as our belt, righteousness as our breastplate, and faith as our shield, we can face anything confidently. If Jesus is raised from the dead, anything by God's grace can become blessing.

No, it's far more than our minds that have to be made up with this story; it's our lives. For in this event is a summons to abandon the way of fear and to take on the way of imperishable hope. Richard Steele tasted this grace when he was about to be jailed for refusing to serve in the South African Defense Force. Walter Wink, in his book *Engaging the Powers* (Augsburg Fortress, 1992), tells his story. Steele, facing the question, "Am I prepared to die for what I believe?" came to this awareness.

> *I realized finally that I was, and this freed me of a tremendous anxiety... The power of fearlessness is astonishing. I think of those who were giving me orders. They were under a real tyranny and far more the victim of it*

> than I was. When they were yelling their orders at me, I had a vivid image of these tiny creatures assaulting my feet, wanting to demolish me with orders, while I was way above, not on their level at all....This was immensely liberating to me, I could be the person I was without fearing them. They had no power over me at all (p. 163).

But if the resurrection is only a summons into this way of courage, then the burden of follow-through is squarely on our shoulders. And we need not do much self-examination to fall into fear again, for we know how inadequate we are to live up to such a call. Tonight I want to state unequivocally to you, however, that Jesus' glorious breakthrough to new life on Easter morning is not merely a summons into the life of fearlessness, but is also the very empowering of it. We are not left to our own resources in this showdown with the powers and principalities. For every time we come here and are stirred by the story, given to praise, enlightened by the word, strengthened by prayer, fed from this table, we tap into resurrection power. This power does wondrous things, amazing things...animating in us reserves of boldness that can face down any challenge, no matter how fearsome.

This power of the resurrection is communicated in a story reported by Brennan Manning in his book *The Lion and the Lamb*. Shortly after the Bolshevist Revolution, Comrade Lunachatsky was lecturing to seven thousand Russian people on the folly of Christianity in contrast to the wisdom of Marxist ideology. All Christian doctrines, he claimed, are empty myths intended to make the poor just accept their fate, and the rest to be anesthetized against seeing reality. "Religion is the opium of the people," he announced. Lunachatsky spoke brilliantly, powerfully, persuasively, and at length. Greatly pleased with himself when the speech was over, he asked if anyone amongst the seven thousand would care to comment on or add to his oratory. A twenty-six-year-old newly ordained Orthodox priest stepped forward, apologized to the commissar for his awkwardness and lack of eloquence, but asked if he could respond. The commissar looked at him skeptically and replied: "You've got two minutes, have at it."

"Oh, I won't take long," the priest assured him. He approached the platform, turned to the audience, and in a clear voice spoke four words. "Christ is risen. Alleluia!" It is reported that the vast audience, as if they were one person, roared in response, "He is risen indeed. Alleluia!"

"Be not afraid," said the angel that gruesome morning, "for I know you seek Jesus who was crucified. He is not here, for he has risen."

Tuning the Senses, Shaping the Resonance

"Be not afraid," says the angel to us, "for I know you seek Jesus who was crucified. He is not here, for he has risen."

Fear nothing, my friends at Christ Church. Resurrection power is erupting once again. Christ is risen! Alleluia!

Karen Johnson serves Christ Episcopal Church in Rockville, Maryland.

How Can This Be?

Lisa Cressman

Have you ever thought about this question of Mary's? As one of my New Testament professors used to say, "Many bottles of exegetical ink have been spilled" as scholars have tried to explain why Mary asked this particular question. Spiritual, psychological, and contextual explanations abound. It may surprise you that there's been so much discussion about a simple and apparently logical question. But the problem is, there's no reason for Mary to have asked this question.

So far, Gabriel has told Mary only that she has been chosen to give birth to a son, the son whom God favors to take the throne of David and rule forever. There's no reason at this point for Mary to think other than that she has just landed the "Big Kahuna" of Jewish motherhood: she would give birth to the King who would fill the vacant spot in the reign of King David. It was every Jewish woman's dream to be the mother of the King who would save God's chosen people from political tyranny. Furthermore, there is no reason for her to think that Joseph wouldn't be the father. She's engaged to him, and he is of David's lineage. Joseph is the link for the Davidic monarchy to resume, a lineage that will hold God's greatest blessings for success.

So, why does she ask, "How can this be?"

I won't attempt to offer you all the explanations through the centuries, but there is one consistent theme. It's not so much that Mary needs to ask the question; it's that we, those who would hear this story retold throughout the ages, we need to hear the answer. It's not that Mary has a problem with the concept of God doing whatever God wants to do. We're the ones who have trouble with it. We're the ones who have trouble believing that "nothing is impossible with God." The question then, "How can this be?" is not asked for Mary's benefit, it's asked for ours.

We're still asking the question. "How can this be?" "How can this be," that God enters the world as an infant? "How can this be," that God can care about us enough to become one of us? "How can this be," that God would choose a young girl of no consequence to be the ultimate servant and bearer of our salvation? "How can this be," that the Infinite chooses to take on the limitations of the finite for our well being? "How can this be," that the birth of God has anything to do with us, or with the salvation of the world?

This question can feel all the more pointed and poignant during this season of the year. It's a difficult season for many people. For most folks, it's at least a very hectic season. For all of us, it's the darkest, gloomiest time of the year with the shortest amount of daylight. There are many pressures, as some scramble to pay outrageous sums of money for that last-to-be-found "Tickle Me Elmo," or as they try to spend more than their credit cards allow. Our houses are supposed to look cheerful, we're supposed to have family to create the Norman Rockwell fantasy; and we're supposed to be full of nothing other than anticipation and good cheer. For many, many of us, the "supposed to's" only make real life feel all the worse. In the face of large debt, disappointed children, family tension or lack of family, and exhaustion, many of us will ask the question, "How can this be," that this is supposed to be the happiest season of all?

Surely, it was not a happy season for Mary. Great dangers lay ahead of her as she negotiated a pregnancy out of wedlock. There was no money, and apparently no family for her to turn to. Then there is an unexpected journey to return to Joseph's hometown of Bethlehem for them to be counted in a mandatory government census. Mary must have asked herself during her arduous travels and pregnancy, "How can this be: I am God's favored one, and this is how I'm treated?"

One Christmas in particular I asked myself, "How can this be the happiest season of all?" I was twenty-four years old, working the twelve-hour day shifts of Christmas Eve and Christmas Day as a registered nurse on the surgical intensive-care unit at the University of Utah Hospital. My patient was a nineteen-year-old Caucasian man. In the early-morning hours of December 24, he hanged himself in the basement of his father's home. His father found him before he died, and he was brought to the hospital where I worked. By the time I arrived for the day shift on the morning of the twenty-fourth, he was engulfed in tubes, wires, and a ventilator, as we tried to bring him back to life.

By the morning of the twenty-fifth it became clear that this beautiful young man was not going to live. The next question was whether or not we could help him live long enough to become an organ donor. As healthy as he was, most of his organs could be used to help someone else live a healthier and maybe much longer life. The young man's father was willing for his son to become a donor, and would sign the necessary papers...but he was not willing to visit his son. The father didn't disclose the reason why he wouldn't see his son, but we talked several times by phone that day. The father said he didn't know why his son would have done this to himself.

In order to keep this young man alive, we had to give him many strong drugs. It was a balancing act all that eternally long day to give him enough medication so that he would live long enough to be a donor, without giving him so many drugs that his organs were ruined by the toxicity of the medications. By the time twilight fell, we knew that we had lost even this second battle. Not only could we not save this man's life, the drugs needed to sustain his life had wrecked his organs. The only thing that could be used were his corneas.

I remember standing at the floor-to-ceiling windows that overlooked the Salt Lake City Valley. I felt utterly defeated. I fought back tears of anger and frustration at the waste: a waste of a life full of potential, and a waste of the benefits of organs that others may have received. It was all a waste, and my efforts along with it. I wondered what in God's name I was doing there. Why wasn't I being introduced to this young man, whole and healthy, in one of those houses I could see in the valley? I knew that families and friends were gathered together in those warmly lit homes to share the celebration of Christ's birth, to eat and laugh, tell stories, and open presents. How could it be that I was standing there working like the devil for this tragic ending of a life, while at the same time joy and laughter and feasting...and the birth of the Savior...carried on. I just couldn't hold together such depth of sorrow and such heights of joy.

I wasn't alone in my questions. Gabriel gave Mary a promise. And Mary asked, "How can this be?" on behalf of the countless people who would wonder the same thing. How can this promise be? How can this promise be made real, come to life, be realized? That was my question on that Christmas ten years ago: How can this be that the promise that Gabriel offered was real? How could the promise of the birth of the Savior, the King of Kings, the Redemption of the World be real, while I stood at this man's bedside in grief and frustration?

But the promise was made real, in a stable in Bethlehem. It was made real when the promise came to life in a shriek and a cry, in blood and tears, in horrible, smelly conditions, while at the same time others rested comfortably in an inn just a few steps away. The promise lived and ate and suckled and cooed, even while a few weeks after his birth babies would be put to death in an effort that King Herod made to destroy the promise of the King of Kings who was made reality. The promise came alive in our Redeemer Jesus Christ, just to show us that it is so. The fulfilled promise makes real that the joy of celebration redeems the speechless grief of death; that security in God's love redeems the fear of financial ruin; that compassion of Christ redeems the loneliness of not having a family; and the impossible reality of Christ redeems the seeming futility of one more attempt to reconcile with our family members.

How can it be that God could promise and fulfill so very much? How can the promise be fulfilled during pain and doubt and fear and tragedy? We need to hear the answer: The promise is fulfilled because of the Holy Spirit, and the power of the Most High. It can be so because the child is born and is holy and is exalted, and is the Most High God. How can this be? We still need to hear the answer. It can be so…it is so…because nothing is impossible with God.

Lisa Cressman serves Trinity Episcopal Church in Indianapolis, Indiana.

A Bean Taco and a Cup of Coffee

Sylvia Vasquez

Jesus said: "As I have done for you, so should you do for one another: Serve others and eat and drink in remembrance of me."

Why is today called Maundy Thursday? Maundy is a derivative of mandate. Today we receive our mandate or commandment from Jesus. The great commandment is this: that we love God and one another as God loves us.

On that last night they were together, some very remarkable things happened to Jesus and the disciples in the upper room. Now, the actual activities were pretty mundane: They washed up, and then they ate, and they drank. But the significance of those mundane actions took on a deeply profound meaning when Jesus reinterpreted those acts in light of his impending death.

The bread and the wine became his body and blood; these sacred elements are the nourishment that give us the strength to walk in the footsteps of Jesus. The washing of the feet became the model for discipleship; this humble symbolic act reminds us that we are to be servants to one another.

Why these things, why the use of such common, basic, everyday food and mundane acts?

One day a few years ago, I was experiencing a crisis in my life. My world seemed to be crumbling around me; I felt abandoned, betrayed, misunderstood, lost. I went to my church to try to get a handle on the downward spiral my life was taking. I thought: "If I can get to church and sit in quiet and gather myself, maybe I can find the strength to go on with my life." I was depending on God to give me the courage and the wisdom to know what to do.

In my anxiety and pain, I sat in front of the life-size crucifix, and tried to pray. I was unable to formulate much beyond a series of complaints against God. As my anxiety increased, and my feelings of being abandoned by God mounted, I became very angry with God. I began to blame God for all my troubles. I confronted God with all the anger and pain I was feeling. Finally, in exasperation and frustration, I stood and shook my fist and screamed aloud: "What good are you to me, hanging there on the cross, constantly reminding me that you died your horrible death. What about now, where are you now?! I need you here with me, not up there, doing nothing but dying, always dying!" I slumped back in the pew, exhausted, and feeling defeated. Ironically, in my exhaustion my mind finally was quieted enough for God to speak to my heart. The message I received was this: "I am with you right now. Every day I am with you, and I have always been with you. When you are ready, you will one day understand and know it in your heart."

Years later, I was working for an agency that ministers to women who have served prison time. I was the director of the agency, and the only full-time staff member. The troubles of the women and the lack of resources to meet their needs were heavy on my mind all the time.

One morning I was on my way to the food bank to pick up our weekly portion for the women, but I was too early. Not wanting to go back to the office to face the women and their enormous problems, I decided to stop and get something to eat. Because of the intensity and pervasive nature of the problems the women faced, I rarely had the opportunity to eat a leisurely meal, so I was happy for the unexpected breather.

Normally, if I have time, I enjoy a hearty meal, but that morning, instead of ordering an elaborate breakfast, I decided that I wanted a bean taco and a cup of coffee.

Now, you can't get a much simpler meal in San Antonio than a bean taco and cup of coffee. And it was an unusual order for me since I am not a coffee drinker, and I am very picky about my refried beans. But in my worried mood about the problems of the women I sensed a deep longing for simple food, so when the waitress asked me for my order, I found myself saying, "A bean taco and a cup of coffee, please."

I waited for my food, and I sat there and grumbled to God about the sorry state of the women's lives, and the even sorrier response of the larger community that was being so stingy in its support for the work we were trying to accomplish. I was in the midst of some pretty serious grumbling when my food arrived. I continued to grumble and gripe to God as I took my first bite of the taco.

I began to chew as I continued to harangue God, when I was overwhelmed by a profound sense of love. I felt as though someone I had been waiting for all my life had arrived and was holding me and comforting me. I took another bite of the taco, and tried to go back to my litany of complaints.

But the second bite of the taco produced a feeling of gratitude and plenitude. I felt so blessed to be Mexican American, so blessed to have that wonderfully simple food that gave so much to me. I was transported back to my childhood. I remembered my Abuelita Petra and her tortillas and beans: gold and light brown griddle marks on soft white flour tortillas, filled with slightly mushed refried beans, with the perfect blend of garlic and bacon pieces. I was not close to her, but I knew my grandmother loved me because she always had hot tortillas and fresh beans ready for me when I came to her house. I thought—what is it? Why is this terribly ordinary food producing such wildly exalted thoughts and feelings?

I was overwhelmed with love at the beauty of my culture, my heritage, my family. And because I knew and had experienced the reality of that love and care, I also knew that God cared and loved me. I know this sounds strange and maybe even funny; but I felt God's presence in that taco. I knew that God was with me and would always be with me and had been with me all along. The memory of the day I yelled at the crucifix came back to me in a flash; and then I understood the message I had received all those years ago.

Knowing that God was present, and more importantly, actually experiencing God's presence with me that morning, energized me for the work of the Kingdom. Because I had been nourished and fed, I felt the courage and energy to face my difficult work. I was ready to wash the feet of the women I served. I was even ready and willing to wash the feet of the bureaucrats who control the funds I needed to continue in the ministry to the women.

That's why we remember today the institution of the Holy Eucharist and the washing of the feet together. One helps us have the strength to do the other. We need the nourishment of the Eucharistic Feast in order to do the work of the Kingdom.

The Holy Communion is not for the worthy and holy, it is for the weak and sinful. We come to the table of the Lord for strength, we are not invited to the banquet as a reward. In Eucharistic Prayer "C" the final prayer is this: "Deliver us from the presumption of coming to this Table for solace only, and not for strength; for pardon only, and not for renewal." We come to the altar because the Holy Communion is meant for all baptized Christians, sinful or not, worthy or not, ready or not.

Pieces of the mystery of God's presence were revealed to me in that taco, and I came to understand that sometimes it is through the gift of the most basic and simple food and events that we can actually experience God. The trauma of my crisis all those years ago has long since faded in light of the really hard times I have had to face in recent years with the death of my brother and mother.

Yet, because God spoke to me in the ordinariness of my food, I have had the courage to face the difficulties of my life. Jesus chose ordinary bread and common wine as a memorial of his life, death, and resurrection. God speaks to us through those sacred elements in the hope that we will be willing servants to continue the work of God's reign. God is always trying to reach out to us in the way that we might best hear and understand. Our mandate has been given to us this day, in the simple actions of our Lord and Savior. When we eat this bread and drink this cup, let us remember the example of Jesus when he washed the feet of his disciples.

In light of all this, we can say: "Of course Jesus chose bread and wine. Of course Jesus is really present." The question is, having been nourished by the bread and wine, can we be present to the reality of Jesus all around us, in the needs of the stranger, in the troubles of the other? Can we celebrate the presence of Jesus in the air, the bluebonnets, the baby crying, the everyday food of our lives?

And once we do believe that Jesus is present to us in this way, can we then respond in love, service, and compassion to those we come in contact with every day? Let us this day, this Holy Day of Remembrance, say *yes* to the Great Commandment: Love one another as I have loved you. Amen.

Sylvia Vasquez serves St. Paul's Episcopal Church in San Antonio, Texas.

The Difficulty of Decreasing

William Hethcock
John 3:25–30

John's disciples are upset. They are worried. You might even say they have a mad on. One day, a while back, Jesus showed up where John was baptizing, and John actually told everyone that Jesus was greater than he. What really gets to them is John's words. "He must increase, but I must decrease." His disciples are thinking that John made a big mistake, because his followers, his clientele, those who have come to him there in the wilderness, are now going over to this other person, this Jesus, and becoming his followers.

John's disciples are running scared. "He must increase, but I must decrease." They're thinking, "John, you have messed up a really good thing."

We would like to think they played together when they were kids, these two little boys Jesus and John, cousins because their mothers were related. Jesus lived over in Nazareth with his parents, Joseph and Mary. And John, the son of Elizabeth and Zechariah, lived in the hill country of Judah. If you move out smartly, it's a possible walk on a good day.

Prior to the birth of their children, Mary had hurried over to see Elizabeth for some girl talk. Both expecting mothers had a story to tell. Elizabeth was in her old age when she realized what was about to happen; and Mary, alas, wasn't even married. Even though both Zechariah and Joseph seemed to be managing their surprises fairly well, these two women clearly needed each other. It was the kind of social situation that will bond two families.

And so, I have no difficulty imagining those two boys playing with each other when they were growing up. John got dropped off at Nazareth during one of Zechariah's turns as a priest in the Temple. They both knew how to tease. John hid his uncle's tools in the carpenter shop just to see what Joseph would do, and Jesus put a frog in the drawer where Mary kept all those blue veils she always wore. They ran in the fields, heckled the sheep, dropped smooth stones in the well to hear the splash, and accomplished rather reluctantly the chores assigned them. The two were active, bright, mischievous, endearing, and promising.

John and Jesus were equals then.

Every now and then, they doubtless were overcome by a strange sober moment. It happened more often as they grew older. They would stop what they were doing, these two boys, John and Jesus, and an unaccustomed moment of dead seriousness would pass between them, a wordless transaction between two companions wondering at their increasing self-awareness. It was as if they were coming to know somehow that their futures were foreordained. Something was going to be required of them; and John and Jesus would, regardless of whatever, fulfill those expectations.

Later on, as even good friends sometimes do, they drifted apart. John became an ascetic, a solitary monastic of sorts, a hermit, living in the wilderness beyond the Jordan River, dressing strangely, eating a sparse diet, and telling those who came to visit him that they were no better than a family of snakes. In spite of his lack of hospitality, many came to him to receive his baptism. He convinced them to submit to being dunked into the dirty waters of the Jordan, and he promised them that when they came out of the river, their clothes sticking to their bodies and their hair matted with mud, their repentance would prepare them for a new age. The new age would include a special preacher, he said, one mightier than the charismatic recluse, John.

This one who was coming had an even more powerful baptism, John announced. Even if against their better judgment, John's motley flock was being prepared for something tremendous, something that would surpass what their imaginations could conjure.

John's cousin Jesus went along a different path. He took a shine to studying the scriptures; and his talent for learning pointed him toward the rabbinate. Word of his vocation went around Nazareth. Mary and Joseph were proud of Jesus, if a little puzzled by his indefinite plans. They wondered at his introspection, his serious prayer, his willingness to confront firmly though clearly without abrasion.

Jesus left his parents. He went off on his own to follow his bliss, to honor his own strong inner drives, to surrender to the heavenly voice coming to him from deep within himself. He seemed to surrender his own sense of self-concern and to focus his attention on those around him. Jesus the man became the epitome of selflessness.

He showed up one day on the bank of the river where John was standing waist-deep in that water, dunking the penitent and sending their sins floating downstream. Cousin John showed no surprise at Jesus' arrival, even though he let everyone know that he had been waiting for him a long time. "Among you stands one whom you do not know," John told the crowd, "the one who is coming after me; I am not worthy to untie the thong of his sandal." This was when this "decrease" idea first showed itself.

The next day John saw Jesus coming toward him and declared, "Here is the Lamb of God who takes away the sin of the world! I saw the Spirit descending from heaven like a dove, and it remained on him. This is he of whom I said, 'After me comes a man who ranks ahead of me because he was before me.' He must increase, but I must decrease."

All those things took place a while back now. A good deal has happened to Jesus since his appearance with John. He has gathered his own disciples, actually some of them from John's entourage. Jesus has encountered the religious authorities. He has changed water into wine, and he has enjoyed a rabbinical disputation with Nicodemus. News of all this is getting around, and some of John's remaining disciples are hearing about it.

They say to John, "That person who was with you, the one you witnessed about. Remember? The one the white bird landed on. Guess what we've heard, Rabbi. We've heard that he is actually doing his own baptizing these days, and he is doing it in Judea. It's a small-town movement now; but with the strong following he is gaining, there is no telling what he will be able to do in Jerusalem. And wouldn't you know, Rabbi John, our followers are going over to him. And we know why this is happening, John. It's because of what you said, 'He must increase, but I must decrease.'" And then his disciples try to explain to John, "You know, it's very hard to work for someone who is trying to decrease himself."

"Well," Rabbi John says to them, "you know, that's the way it's going to be. I've been trying to tell you, and you don't get it. You see," John is saying quite earnestly now, "our ministry only has value to God when it is aimed at preparing men and women for someone beyond ourselves. Our ministry only prepares people for his ministry. We must turn our attention from ourselves to him. He must increase, and not only must I decrease, but so must all of you."

Oh, my goodness! Decrease, you say? The word you have for us, Rabbi John, is no better for us than it is for your disciples. All of us are looking for our own place in the system, and you're telling us you're downsizing. That's not what we have in mind, John.

We caught up with Jesus the other day, and we tried to explain to him that decreasing is not possible right now, but he was busy and couldn't listen to us. He appeared to be washing someone's feet. We were trying on new vestments in the sacristy the other day, and they all seemed just grand, until we caught a glimpse of the crucifix; and then the clothes seemed, well, not right, maybe even uncomfortable. You see, we know we entered this seminary thing with vocation in mind, but we're learning more recently that it's necessary also to think package.

Don't get us wrong, Rabbi John. We believed what you said when you spotted Jesus on the riverbank. We know that he is greater and all. We know about the bird coming down and the voice. And we believe all that. We talk about Lamb of God and that kind of thing all the time. We are believers here, John.

In fact, some of us have known Jesus for a long time. We grew up together. We knew Jesus when. Jesus encouraged us to grow and learn and love and follow him. We are on our way. And decreasing is not a part of the program God gave us. Is it?

Good friends, what it comes down to is this. It's a question of humility. We decrease by becoming humble. In the face of Jesus' generosity, benevolence, sacrifice, and self-giving, Jesus increases, because he is the Christ of God. We, then, must decrease, and it is a question of humility.

John's disciples were coming at him with jealousy and fear. They were making it difficult for him. Humility is always difficult, especially when those around us are telling us we're great. But decreasing is the only thing that is appropriate. Humility becomes a follower of Christ. John knew it, and he was going to live as a follower of Christ, even if it cost him his life. And it did.

Being humble servants may be the hardest challenge we have. No one graduates from seminary and gets ordained without a sense of personal accomplishment and pride. No one puts on a clerical collar without hoping that everyone will notice. No one gets called by a special title without feeling a little elevated above the masses. No one preaches a sermon without hoping some people will say how swell it was. No one visits the hospital without hoping the patient's family will say thank you. No one struggles with family and children to make it on a really inadequate salary without being a little proud of the misery and sacrifice.

Decreasing is hard work. Humility is a commodity that costs more than we know how to pay.

The irony is that we think we know how it ends. The moment will come when our earthly life is over. However we sift through the lore that surrounds that moment, we suspect strongly that we will see Jesus face to face. He will be weeping when we lift our heads and dare to glance into his eyes.

But a wry grin will begin to develop there. Jesus will say to us in one way or another, "You didn't make it in the decreasing department, did you? But you gave it a shot, and I'm making up your deficit. You are forgiven, reconciled, saved, and free. Come on in. The heavenly banquet is under way, and I have a seat of honor for you at the head table next to me."

I ask you. In the face of a welcome like that, how can we do anything but decrease?

William Hethcock is Professor of Homiletics, Emeritus, the School of Theology of the University of the South in Sewanee, Tennessee.

I Was a Son of Sceva

James Adams
Acts 19:11–20

Paul's ministry was born of a confrontation. On the road to Damascus, Paul was struck to the ground in a flash and confronted...confronted by Christ himself. After that, everything was different for Paul. Everything. No distance was too far to travel with the Gospel in hand. No person, no demon, no disease could avoid being confronted by Paul, since he had been confronted by Christ. No wonder God's healing power flowed so freely through his hands.

For the Seven Sons of Sceva, it was a another story. Sceva's boys were very good customers of the Wippell Company—haberdashers to the holy. No doubt they looked terrifically holy.... No doubt, when they spoke it was in deep, resonant church tones.

Sceva's boys heard about the miracles God was doing through Paul. So, when they are ready to do an exorcism, they speak directly to the evil spirit. "I adjure you by the Jesus Paul proclaims," they shout. But, as soon as they speak, all hell breaks loose.

The evil spirit turns to the Sons of Sceva, "Jesus I know. Paul I know. But who are you?" (Jack Kennedy was a friend of mine and Senator, you're no Jack Kennedy.) The pretty boys fall flat on their backs, wearing nothing but their mail-order miters.

The scene closes, the credits start to roll, and you just want to cheer, don't you? After all, Paul is our guy, a Christian...one of us. The Sons of Sceva are the bumbling bad guys who only pretend. Good guys and bad guys. If only it were so easy.

Working as a chaplain at Georgetown University Hospital, I prided myself on being the young, energetic "God guy" on the seventh floor. I was trying out the look and the language of priesthood and I was liking it. I was a Son of Sceva. Patients with serious diseases asked me to pray for them. They were searching for the healing power of God and hoped that I held some of that power in my hands.

But I was playing it safe. When I prayed to God, I was careful not to ask for too much. I didn't want them to get their hopes up. I was afraid to pray for anything too big because I trusted God too little.

It was while I was galloping from room to room in the hospital that I ran into a doctor who asked me to look in on a forty-seven-year-old patient whose name was Frances. He said that her heart was very weak and deteriorating quickly. He said that she probably had only a couple of weeks to live. He also said that she had AIDS and that her family had abandoned her. "She could use a friend," he said. "She could use a friend."

I trotted down to her room. Frances was sleeping when I walked in and when I walked out...fast. She had been devastated by disease. Her body was like a skeleton draped with skin. I was scared. Her bruised and bony arms and legs were covered with open sores. She looked as though she had been beaten and left to die alone. I got out of there fast. "Please let her know that I stopped by," I told the nurse on my way out. "I'll come back when she's awake."

I was not coming back. On my own, I could not. I abandoned her there. Her need was too great and my faith was too small. I could not do anything for her. I was a Son of Sceva.

Day after day, I visited all the patients on the seventh floor...all except one. Day after day, the vision of Frances all alone wore me down. Two weeks dripped by. I was devastated by what I had not done. I met with a priest and confessed my sin to God. The priest prayed for me...hands were placed on my head.

Frances was still holding on to life. I would go see her and talk with her honestly. She was sleeping when I walked in and sat nervously beside her bed. This time, I stayed with her. After a few minutes, Frances opened her eyes. In a flash, I was struck from my high horse. I was confronted by Christ, Christ in the flesh, right before my eyes. "You are my priest," Frances said. "No, I'm a chaplain," I corrected her. "I knew my priest would come to see me. I'm so glad you came," she said.

"Frances, I was afraid. I was afraid to come see you," I whispered. She closed her eyes. "Because I look so sick?" she asked. I nodded..."Yes. How human." That's what she said.

"How human." Sweet forgiveness. And then it was silent for a moment or an hour...I'm not sure. And then she began to speak.

She told me about how she got sick and about her struggle to get well. She told me how her family had fallen apart. She had not seen her son, Nathan, or her daughter, Ellen, in over a year. The doctors had told her that time was running out. In her despair, she had turned to God. She thought about heaven where her body would be made well... where broken relationships would be healed. "I'd like another chance at being a mom," she said.

"Jesus is going to rescue me...make me whole again," she said.

"Do you mean in heaven, Frances? Do you mean that Jesus will make you whole again in heaven?" I asked, hoping the answer was yes.

"I know that he will do that. But I want to get well. I hope to live," she answered. And that is when she asked the question, "Jim, will you hold my hands and pray with me that Jesus will rescue me?"

Did I believe that Jesus could or would rescue her from a certain and imminent death through my hands? What did I believe about healing? Did it matter at that moment? What was God doing? What was God doing with Frances and with me?

Healing is God's work. It is God's mysterious labor of love. Once confronted by Christ, our lives and our ministry are forever a "hands-on" mission with power beyond our understanding. Healing runs through us and to us. The Spirit moves...the sick are made well, broken relationships are renewed, awakening to God begins.

You probably want to know what happened to Frances. We spent time talking and praying together, nearly every day, for five weeks. I wish that I could tell you that she was cured of disease. She was not.

But healing did happen. One day, Frances had a family visitor. The first in a year. Without notice, her son, Nathan, came to visit and he brought his mother flowers. And there was more: On August 5, 1995, against the advice of her doctors, Frances checked herself out of the hospital. Today, more than a year later, she is living...somehow living at home in Washington, D.C. The nurse who cares for her every day is her daughter, Ellen.

Was there a miracle in Georgetown? Frances's story of healing is hers to explain. For me the answer is yes. Yes, God did extraordinary miracles through Frances. The forces that brought fear, that dampened my faith in God were made powerless, at least for a time. I witnessed the healing power of God up close. I was confronted...confronted by Christ in that flesh and I was healed.

James Adams serves St. Thomas Episcopal Church in Hanover, New Hampshire.

Preaching in Idea Form

Flying Saucers, UFOs, and Alien Invasions
Leander Harding

Tonight I am going to talk about something that may seem strange as a topic for a Christmas Eve sermon. I am going to talk about flying saucers, UFOs, and alien invasions. My job is to tell the story of Jesus Christ. In order to tell the story of Jesus Christ effectively it is important to listen to the other stories that people tell each other. People express their hopes and fears in the stories they tell. Tonight the church proclaims that, in Jesus Christ, the hopes and fears of all the years have been met. The stories of UFOs and space aliens have a form which seems strange, even bizarre to some; but the content of these stories is familiar and universal. At the heart of these stories the human heart cries out in hope and fear. I want to spend a few moments exploring these stories in order to suggest that the true and living story of the birth of the Savior is the answer to the desire of the human heart being expressed by this fascination with visitors from outer space.

Isn't it interesting that stories of visitors from outer space persist, and enjoy great popularity, in spite of the obvious scientific difficulties. From a strictly scientific viewpoint it seems plausible that there is life elsewhere in the universe, and implausible, given the vastness of the universe and the limit of the speed of light, that we have been visited by intergalactic travelers. Yet the interest in this topic is huge and television programs and movies which explore these themes have large and enthusiastic audiences. *Close Encounters of the Third Kind, X Files, Third Rock from the Sun, Independence Day, Mars Attacks,* and more that you can name. People do not get tired of telling these stories; and people do not get tired of hearing these stories. Two basic themes are represented.

First there is the alien as a strange and sinister force, immensely sophisticated, which threatens to destroy humanity by a combination of superior force and deceit. Often in these stories, such as the *X Files,* there are traitorous human beings who are willing to aid the evil aliens, and prepare the way for them in the mistaken notion that they can cut a separate deal. Often there are humans who have been completely taken over. They look human, but have been taken over from the inside out, and are really now enemy agents. There are those terrifying scenes where the evil alien creature that has consumed the person from the inside out breaks through the skin of the person, and the horrible truth is revealed. These story lines also have a heroic figure who has learned the horrible truth of imminent destruction and can't get well-intentioned but terminally naive innocents to take him seriously. You sit in the theater saying to yourself, "For God's sake, listen to him before it is too late."

Then there is a another story line, a more hopeful one. The aliens are superior beings, morally and spiritually superior as well as technologically. From time to time they have visited us to help and guide us, to nudge and direct the course of our history. Now the time is right for them to reveal themselves and save us from ecological disaster, planetary war, and destruction. In some versions of this story line, the aliens mate with humans to create a new race, a superior race, morally and spiritually as well as physically. This new race will change the course of the history and give us hope that we might survive.

I believe these stories of visitors from outer space exert a strange power over so many people because they speak of deep intuitions in the human heart. Human beings look at life on planet Earth, and know with a deep intuition that there is a power at work in human affairs that is dark and sinister, and which is underestimated by people. Many good people seem naive and complacent, unheeding of the warning, as the greedy, selfish, and hateful play with forces they do not understand. When will they listen? When will they listen?

It may be hard to believe in flying saucers, but it is not hard to believe that our race, the human race, is a threatened race, our planet a threatened planet, and that the situation calls for dramatic action. These are the kind of things people feel in their bones. This is a deep and true intuition of the human heart. The form of this story may be fantastic, but the content is profound. This story of a threatened people and a threatened world is a more profound story than the story that some combination of science, technology, and commerce will solve all our problems.

The other story line, the more hopeful one, also reflects a profound intuition of the human heart; that there is in the universe a benevolent force that is more powerful than human beings are, a force that is good and which subtly influences history for the positive, a force which is on our side and working to save us and our world. It is also a profound intuition that what has been hidden is about to be revealed, and that what has been working behind the scenes is about to step out onto center stage. Even this seemingly bizarre part about the mating of humans and aliens represents a profound intuition of the human heart. The human heart knows about the reality of the first story, the story of evil which threatens to destroy from the inside out, the story of human stupidity and cupidity in the face of that evil. The human heart knows that there needs to be some new element—new blood, yes, but more importantly a moral and spiritual transfusion leading to a renewed and redeemed humanity. If only this were true, there would be hope. We might make it. We could hold out.

That is the feeling of these stories. While the form is fantasy and the fantastic, the content is deep human truth.

St. Paul the Apostle spoke to the scientific, rational, skeptical, and yet superstitious world of ancient Athens. He spoke to people who were searching and seeking because of a deep feeling that they lacked the moral and spiritual resources to survive. These people had an altar to almost every god imaginable, even to an unknown god. St. Paul said to them, "Men of Athens, that which you worship unknowingly, that it is which I proclaim to you." To a world which expresses its hopes and fears in stories of alien invasion and alien salvation, I want to repeat these words of St. Paul, "that which you worship unknowingly, that it is which I proclaim to you."

I want to say, you are right. There is a sinister and alien force that is stronger and more clever than unaided, unassisted human will and which must be recognized and resisted before it is too late. You are also right that there is a superior, benevolent, beneficent force that guides history, that has been hidden but now wants to be completely known, and to clearly reveal its purposes. This force wants even to have intercourse with human beings and bring to birth a new race with a renewed moral and spiritual power, so that disaster may be forestalled, and we may be saved. This is all true and it is all set forth in the Holy Bible.

There is a good God who means us well, and who guides our history in a subtle way that does not rob us of our freedom or responsibility. There is a force that rebels against God and is bigger, stronger, and more clever than humankind and which threatens to destroy us with the help of our self-defeating connivance. In this dire moment, the good God who has worked behind the scenes has revealed himself, come center stage, to give us direct assistance, again in a way that does not rob us of our freedom or responsibility. The good God, the maker and creator of all things, does this by being born a baby, living and dying as one of us, conquering death, and giving us his life-giving spirit. By joining us to himself in such a way to create a new humanity, reformed, redeemed, renewed by a moral and spiritual infusion.

> *God rest you merry gentlemen, let nothing you dismay;*
> *remember Christ our Savior was born on Christmas Day,*
> *to save us all from Satan's power when we were gone astray*
> *Oh tidings of comfort and joy.*

> *O little town of Bethlehem, how still we see thee lie!*
> *Above thy deep and dreamless sleep the silent stars go by;*
> *yet in thy dark streets shineth the everlasting Light;*
> *the hopes and fears of all the years are met in thee tonight.*

There is a threat and there is a Savior. The Savior is here for us tonight in our Christmas Communion so that he can live in us and we in him, so that he can re-create us as a new and redeemed race capable of honoring and stewarding this world and fit for life beyond the stars with him forever.

Leander Harding serves St. John's Episcopal Church in Stamford, Connecticut.

Of Dogs and Divinity

Stephen Weissman

One of my favorite cartoons shows Linus, Charlie Brown, Lucy, and Snoopy all lined up along a single tree trunk, together in one frame. Linus is saying, "So I had to tell the teacher I didn't know the answer." Charlie Brown is replying, "Some questions you just can't know the answer." Lucy is asking, "Like what?" Snoopy is thinking, "Like, did Jesus have a dog?"

The question does make a person think about dogs and divinity. I have been musing about that topic for the last six weeks; for I have had to have my old Airedale, Clara, put out of her pain. In thanksgiving, therefore, for Clara's fidelity and her good heart, I offer some parallels between on the one hand, our relationship with dogs, and on the other hand, God's relationship with human beings.

Three similarities have come to mind. For one parallel, consider the main reason why a middle-class American keeps a dog at all: companionship. True, some do keep dogs for hunting game, or exterminating vermin, or guarding property. But many more of us keep dogs for their company. Something like that must be why God created human beings, and why God suffers us to remain in his realm. God does not need us. We can mess up his universe. Our yowls to God do not heighten his majesty. God must, therefore, keep us because he likes us around.

For a second parallel, consider the awareness dogs have of their owners. Although dogs depend on us, their understanding of our purposes must be dim. A dog can "make sense" of only a few human actions, still fewer human words, and virtually none of our thoughts. Notwithstanding, dogs do seem to have a vivid grasp of their masters' dispositions. Human apprehension of the divine is similar: We cannot fathom God's thoughts, and we must have God's will impressed upon us repeatedly for us to get it; yet, like dogs seeking their master's attention, we do seek God's attention, we cultivate our awareness of God's disposition toward us. Thus, people must "know" God somewhat like the way dogs must "know" people.

Hence, (this is the third parallel) we act toward God in the ways that dogs act toward us. That is, we defer to God's superiority. We revere God. We seek God's favor to us. We try to conduct ourselves in ways that will avoid his displeasure. Earlier generations would have said that we fear God. In the same way, dogs can be said to fear us.

Having noted those three parallels, I turned to the Bible to see if its authors may have set a precedent in the use of canine imagery to picture the relationship between God and human beings. I was disappointed, for almost every biblical reference to dogs is disparaging. Of all biblical characters, only Tobias (in Tobit) is reported to have had a pet dog, and only Job mentions the use of dogs to guard flocks. Elsewhere in the Hebrew Bible, dogs lick Jezebel's blood. They grin and run about the city. They are described as dumb, greedy, and dead. They are used as an epithet for sodomites and pagans. Equally disparaging, the New Testament uses the term "dog" to insult Gentiles and sorcerers; and Jesus enjoins us not to give to dogs what is holy. The Bible sees dogs as metaphors for human degradation, presumably because dogs were scavengers, not pets, in biblical societies, as pariah dogs are still today in the Middle East. I suspect that the answer to Snoopy's question is, no, Jesus did not own a dog.

Sheep are the animals with which the Bible prefers to compare human beings, and it prefers to compare a shepherd's care for his sheep with God's care for his people. The Psalms alone provide many such comparisons, too familiar to cite. After all, sheep were a major source of income for many in Israel.

So, it is to the Greeks that we must turn for ancient appreciations of the dog. For instance, returning Odysseus spots on his threshold a hound, "Argus was his name, Odysseus himself had owned and trained him, though he had sailed for holy Troy before he could reap the reward of his patience.... [In] his owner's absence, [Argus] lay abandoned.... Directly he became aware of Odysseus' presence, he wagged his tail and dropped his ears, though he lacked the strength now to come any nearer his master. Yet Odysseus saw him...and brushed away a tear...."

Given the Greek tenderness for dogs, it is not surprising that the Hellenization of Christianity likewise "Hellenized" postbiblical Christians' attitudes toward dogs. Thus, by the fourth century, Basil the Great was praising the dog as a paragon of loyalty and gratitude. In the fifth century, Patrick is said to have cared for a boatload of Irish wolfhounds; and, consequently, when a pagan king sicked a wolfhound on Patrick, the dog instead nuzzled the saint's hand, thereby reversing the king's hostility to Patrick's gospel. In the thirteenth century, Dominic assigned his Order of Preachers to be "Canes Domini." In the late Middle Ages, hunting dogs and lap dogs ornamented numerous sacred manuscripts. Later still, Fredrick von Hugel first pointed out in an essay the parallel between our knowledge of God and dogs' knowledge of us. In that same nineteenth century, Francis Thompson wrote a poem characterizing God as the "Hound of Heaven."

The animals of Eden knew their names and they came when Adam called them. Genesis says that Adam and Eve had dominion over the other creatures, just as divine beings had dominion over them. That is, at creation, a divine-human-animal hierarchy was established in which each subordinate being obeyed the superior being, and each superior being was responsible toward its subordinate. Just as in Eden there were no sinful masters, so in Eden there were no bad dogs, either. For both dogs and men, to hear was to obey.

However, when humanity fell from innocence, then all creation was disconnected from us. So the animals no longer came when they were called. Genesis says, "The fear of you and the dread of you shall be on every beast of the earth...." Why? Because the human race failed in obedience. As disobedient beings, we are no longer occupying the relationship of trust with either our Superior or our subordinates, that trust which is the basis of any free obedience. Just as human beings distrust God and violate God's commands, so we become no longer ourselves trustworthy beings; and thus we lose our authority over other creatures. Fear appears then, and vulnerability. We know we are naked; and the animals know we are dangerous. We must coerce them. Dogs slink around our territory, like Adam hiding from God in Eden's shrubbery.

Trust is essential to any relationship, divine, human, or canine. So when trust is dissolved, then masters become indecisive, or else, masters become cruel. A dog belonging to an indecisive master will maneuver and try to usurp mastery for himself whenever he can, ending up as a nuisance. For instance, cartoon dogs such as Marmaduke and Belvedere are creatures of indecisive masters, and thus they are maneuverers.

Dogs of cruel masters either cower or bite. Neither the indecisive master nor the cruel master can exercise dominion in the biblical sense of dominion over his creature. His trustworthiness, and thus his authority, has failed. The human being no longer holds dominion over the animal, because he no longer recognizes himself as someone under a higher authority. Lacking respect for God's commands, fallen humanity no longer respects any commands, and thus we can no longer command respect from the dog. The dog turns disobedient and opportunistic.

An example of someone in such a fallen state is the woman who treats her pooch as responsible for her emotional well-being, as if it were not a dog. She bribes Fido to love her in a way she cannot love herself; she fawns over Fido, feeds Fido junk from the table, neglects to correct Fido, talks baby talk to Fido, and makes the dog obnoxious to anyone who happens into the house. That dog's nature is corrupted. The dog owns no self-respect, because the dog is not trusted to be a dog, just as the mistress has no dignity because she fails to accept her Eve-like authority over the lesser creature. The theological term for their state is depravity. Their house is in disorder. Equally depraved, in a physical way, is the contemptible man who beats his animal into cringing and cowering. A master fallen into cruelty produces a terrified and untrustworthy dog.

Withal, redemption is possible. That is, dogs and dog owners can be trained, and their natures elevated by grace. Grace appears when an owner respects himself enough to restrain himself from expecting the dog to make him happy and/or respects himself enough to be kind to the dog. The good master acts as one in the image of a divine master, and it shows in the way he approaches a dog. The good master commits himself to the dog's better nature. Then, consistently the master uses techniques of correction which good trainers have perfected to name the dog, to bring the dog to recognize the human being's dominion, and to come when called. Good faith is achieved as the dog learns to trust and freely to obey the master.

Finally, off-lead training illustrates the relationship between discipline and freedom, between the law and grace. That is to say, as their training advances, the dog grows in faith in the master, and the master's correction becomes indistinguishable from the dog's self-correction. Ultimately, the master's faith in the dog must be as great as the dog's faith in the master. Then the dog reaches the point where Augustine's dictum is applicable: "Love and do what you will." Other examples of canine natures so fully redeemed might be tracking dogs on whose nose the master must have faith that the dog is smelling what the master cannot, and guide dogs on whose sense of direction the master is entrusting his life. These are the saints of the canine kingdom.

To bring back our analogy once again to God, consider the human beings who trust God so thoroughly that they freely do what God wills. Concomitantly, God has such faith in them that God depends on them to do his will. The ultimate instance of that reciprocal faith is Jesus. Jesus has faith in the Father, and the Father has faith in Jesus. Likewise, a good dog has faith in his master and the master has faith in the dog.

That is why, although the Bible pictures the righteous Israelite with a sheep at his side, I picture the redeemed Adam with a dog beside him. (This sermon was preached on a Sunday close to St. Francis Day.)

Stephen Weissman serves Pike County Episcopal Churches in Louisiana, Missouri.

Life Is Difficult—Come and Live!

John Conrad

M. Scott Peck begins his multimillion-copy bestseller *The Road Less Traveled* with a paraphrase from the Buddha. According to Peck, the Buddha says, "Life is difficult. This is a great truth, one of the greatest truths."

"Life is difficult."

This great truth will probably come as no surprise—no great news—to anyone old enough to have found their way into this church this morning. From the oldest member of our congregation struggling with all the difficulties of aging, to the youngest member of our congregation struggling with new teeth and diaper rash, life is difficult.

To own this fact—that life is difficult—is to have a blessing. We no longer have to spend a lot of time grousing about why life isn't perfect. It can be remarkably helpful and healing to know that life is difficult right now because that's the way life is. In Genesis we hear God saying to Adam, "Cursed is the ground because of you; in toil you shall eat of it all the days of your life; thorns and thistles it shall bring forth for you; and you shall eat the plants of the field. By the sweat of your brow you shall eat bread until you return to the ground, for out of it you were taken; you are dust, and to dust you will return."

From a Christian perspective we can believe that God did not want it to be so. Our Holy Scripture tells of a God who brought the creation into being out of love, who wanted nothing more than to walk with us and talk with us in the garden, in the cool of the day. But we broke our covenant with God, and ever since, life has been difficult. In our present circumstances, to live life is to struggle. It is the work we are all called to do.

It is the premise of Scott Peck's book, as well as the premise of most schools of psychotherapy, that where we as humans come to difficulty is in our failure to face up to the struggle. Peck and the rest say that most of us live in a mode of avoidance—we avoid the struggle and especially we avoid the pain associated with the struggle. Rather than facing up to the challenges that our particular struggle puts before us, we run, hide, make excuses, rationalize, and put the blame on others. Hence, our problems. The man who cannot face his troubled marriage or his troubled job hides himself nightly in a bottle of scotch; the child who cannot face the consequences of a bad report card hides the card in his backpack; the businessman who cannot face the results of poor business performance doctors the books of his business; the treasurer who cannot face the reality of her humble economic status embezzles money from the church; the Navy officer who cannot bear the pain of having never actually been in combat attaches a tiny brass embellishment to an otherwise undistinguished decoration.

Predictably, in each case the situation gets worse. The difficult life becomes more difficult. For the hard drinker, the problems with wife, family, and job become more acute the more he runs and hides and drinks. The hidden report card, when it comes to light, engenders a more severe punishment for the child than it would have otherwise. The hidden financial performance of the business just leads to a postponed but more devastating bankruptcy. The church treasurer who couldn't bear the stigma of a 1,200-square-foot house now finds herself ensconced in an 8x10 prison cell. The sailor who couldn't bear the social pressure of having never been shot at ends up shooting at himself.

Life is difficult. Avoiding the difficulties—avoiding life—always, always makes it more difficult. That which is not addressed initially will always, always be addressed eventually. If you do not go after life then, as Genesis reminds us, life and death will come after you.

This church—any Christian church—runs the risk of making this situation worse instead of better. Because of the nature of this place, we can all easily become unwilling contributors to the problem, instead of individual parts of the solution. The church is a wonderful place to hide—for both laypeople and for the clergy alike. With these high glass windows and cool cement walls, it is easy for us—any and all of us—to come to see this place as a fortress, a bastion, indeed a sanctuary which leaves the problems of the world—our problems—on the other side of the door. However, we are not called to leave our problems outside. We are called to intentionally bring them inside, to know that God loves us and receives us in grace, regardless of our problems.

Thus far I have been talking about the human tendency to avoid difficult problems. As some of you may have noticed, I have been talking about problems and difficulties in general terms instead of referring to a specific problem or difficulty. That's one of the tricks we preachers use to avoid the pain and difficulty of addressing a specific problem. That said, let me summon my courage and present you with a very real problem with which we will all have to deal over the next month or two.

If you have been in church for the last few Sundays, and if you are at all sensitive to this sort of thing, you will have noticed that we are in the process of sidling up on what we Episcopalians euphemistically call a stewardship campaign. You may have noticed the little notices in the bulletin that call your attention to the financial realities of operating this parish church. No doubt you have heard the testimonies of members of our congregation. We are going to hear another one in just a few minutes. However, stewardship is not exactly the problem I'd like to call your attention to. Stewardship points to the problem, but the problem is simply this:

We are told in our Holy Scripture, what we believe to be the revealed word of God, that the tithe is the minimum standard of giving. That is to say that a tenet of the Christian faith, affirmed by the General Convention of the Episcopal Church in 1976, is that Episcopalians—you and I—ought to give ten percent of our total income to the church. The problem is that most of us don't—for a variety of reasons. Some of us cannot give more because we simply don't have the money. Many more of us cannot give more because we have chosen to spend our money, or more accurately we have chosen to spend God's money, on other things. Some of us withhold our money—withhold God's money—because we don't like what the church is doing right now. Which makes all of us—one and all—sinners.

Now that is a problem.

I am not going to offer a solution to this problem this morning. I am going to leave the problem for you to wrestle with during the next few weeks. You should struggle with it. It is supposed to be difficult. But in closing, let me offer some guidance—some advice for your spiritual health and well-being during the struggle.

Don't try to avoid the problem. Don't try to pretend it isn't there. Don't get angry with me for bringing the problem up; don't blame Fr. Mark for calling me to this pulpit; don't blame the vestry for spending too much money. Don't hide, don't run, don't get angry, don't blame.

Rather, give the matter up to God in prayer.

If that sounds a little ethereal to you, let me suggest a practical method—a spiritual discipline that will allow you to do just that. It involves prayer through the use of symbols. First get several small pieces of paper—3x5 cards or the backs of old business cards will do. On the left side of each card, write down the amount you give to the church. On the right side of the card, write down the amount that would be a tithe. For those of you inclined to precision in these matters, that's ten percent of line 20 on your IRS form 1040. Then go and place the pieces of paper strategically around the house or office. Put one on the bathroom mirror, use one for the bookmark in the lurid novel by your bed. If you use a daily prayer book or something like *Forward, Day by Day*...put one of the pieces of paper in there...you get the idea.

Whenever you encounter one of these pieces of paper throughout the day, take a moment, pause, try to be silent, and look at the number on the left side of the paper and allow the figures—the ink on the paper—to become a symbol for who you are right now—a child of God, beloved of God, know that Jesus gave himself up to death on the cross for you—just as you are right now. Then take a look at the figures on the right side of the card and try to see that as a symbol for who you might become—a symbol of who God would have you be. After that, say this simple prayer. "Lord Jesus, I can't do it without your help. Help me." Then wait, watch, listen for the still, small voice of God, and see what happens.

As I hope to exclude no one from the opportunity of feeling uncomfortable about this morning's difficult sermon, I have a final word of caution for those few of you who already tithe. Pride remains the deadliest of the seven deadly sins. In this morning's Gospel Jesus is addressing the chief priests and elders in the temple. He says, "Tax collectors and prostitutes are going into the Kingdom of God before you." Those of us who can identify with the tax collectors and prostitutes—those of us who know our sin—have a blessing. One has to know one's own sin before one can hear the healing message of the Gospel and repent.

This morning we will be using Eucharistic Prayer C—which some of you may find as uncomfortable and unsettling as you have found this sermon. The opening language of that prayer speaks to a modern Christian understanding of God as creator, and those of you who have been attending the adult forum will now hear it with new ears. The prayer is challenging in that it requires considerable participation from the congregation. In order to pray the Great Thanksgiving, it will be necessary for you to follow along in the book and make the appropriate responses. Beyond all this the prayer is exceedingly appropriate for this morning because it contains these words: "Open our eyes to see your hand at work in the world about us. Deliver us from the presumption of coming to this Table for solace only, and not for strength, for pardon only and not for renewal."

So come to the altar now—come for renewal. Come to the altar for solace and pardon—but also come to the altar for strength. You will need your strength. Life is difficult. This is a great truth...one of the greatest truths. Life is difficult. Come to the altar and live.

John Conrad serves St. Mark's Episcopal Church in Glendale, California.

Tickle Me

Richard McCandless

"Be not afraid.... To you is born this day a savior, who is Christ the Lord."

"Tickle me" is the word this Christmas. A little luck, good timing, and careful promotion have made a ticklish fuzzy toy named Elmo the hit of Christmas 1996.

Other than our dogs and people who haven't had their first birthday yet, it's my policy never to tickle anyone who isn't a relative by blood or marriage. If you tickle the wrong person you'll need quick reflexes or a good trial attorney. But watch people's faces when a baby laughs, or even when a mechanical toy laughs. You'll see delight and warmth in the most cautious and discreet people.

Laughing makes us equal. Laughter brings people close quickly. It's hard to walk by a room where people are laughing without listening in to hear why. I heard an expert on schools say he can tell who the best teachers are just by walking the halls and finding the rooms where kids are laughing. Laughter is a good indication of a workplace where people are doing good things.

I think "Tickle Me Elmo" is successful because he's medicine against the fear that life is getting too complicated to be fun, and too isolated for us to be close to each other. He's not competitive. He's not frustrating. He's just fun. And he's about thirty bucks, if you can find him.

So, instead of being trivial, the success of that toy points to simple and important things.

What people want to hear from the Church at Christmas is something simple they can use to answer their basic questions. Peter Gomes, who teaches at Harvard, has written a good popular book about simple, fundamental questions and the Bible. At book-signing events he meets people who, he says, "are prepared to exchange the Good Life for the life that is good." They're asking "How?" —they want some basic directions.

We who have a thoroughly scientific and material mind struggle with things in the Bible, things like a virgin birth and a choir of angels. They sound like relics of an obsolete world. Knowing that, let's see if we can deal with something simple and fundamental. It's about one of the things the Church knows and which is connected with our celebration of Christmas. It's about community.

Let's begin where Jesus began, in first-century Hebrew society. Their traditions and holy books were full of a kind of story called midrash, which is simply the creative application of old themes to new needs. The Gospel of Luke is using midrash when it pictures Jesus' birth as strikingly similar to well-known stories about King David, the patriarch Isaac, and the strongman Samson, stories which first-century readers recognized in Luke's account of Christmas.

The point is not the details. Anyone who insists that the details fit science is going to be frustrated. Matthew's Gospel puts the point in one word, "Emmanuel," which literally means "God-with-us." The point is, this is the story of God's coming very close to us, and therefore of our getting very close to God, and to each other. It's the story of the start of a community.

Religion in America is polarized between two extremes today. On the one hand there's the religious world of the big old institutions, populated by church officials and their assistants. This institutional world holds less and less interest for most people. While some of my colleagues complain about that, I'm not sure it isn't a good thing. A college chaplain compares the denominational hierarchy to "an aged dowager, living in a decaying mansion on the edge of town, bankrupt and penniless, house decaying around her, but acting as if her family still controlled the city."

On the other hand, there's the religious life of individual people. Often it's completely personal, either by choice or by accident. In the movie *The Ruling Class* a mental patient claims to be God. The psychiatrist asks him when he first found out he was God. He answers, "I was praying and praying for years, then one day I woke up and discovered I was only talking to myself!"

Between the old but irrelevant institution and the personal search, there's nothing in the middle for lots of people. There's a gap between the big institution over there and the individual over here, and we have a sense that something should be there in that space, but what? This year there was a debate in American intellectual circles over the suggestion of Robert Putnam that there is a wholesale dying out of all the small associations of people that bridge the gap between individuals and institutions.

Sometimes we just dismiss the question. But every now and then, in a particular place, a church, a school, a college, or a group of some kind is so good at bringing us together and giving us a vision, that it becomes real and powerful. For the people who are fortunate to be part of it, it fills that gap. They become more than tourists—they become a community.

Bigger than an individual alone, but not so big as to be out of sight, these are communities in the best sense. They are places where people are close to each other, and God is close to them. They are down-to-earth examples of what the Christmas stories in the Gospels were driving at—incarnation. These communities become places where people care about, and for, each other.

Someone asked Margaret Mead what was the first evidence of civilization in any culture. They expected her to point to a tool or a technology. She said, "A broken femur that's healed again." "Why a broken bone?" they asked. "Because," she said, "the fact that someone had broken a leg and lived while it healed proved that someone else took care of them; someone else did their hunting, kept them warm, brought them water while the broken leg healed. That shows compassion," she said, "and where there was compassion there was civilization."

They also become places where people search and find. If you are searching for an honest and healthy spiritual life, and if you're tired of being sorted by zip code as a consuming unit and marketed to someone else, then what Christianity and St. Paul have to give you is this experience of community, where incarnation happens. This parish is one of the rare places where that is happening genuinely. To find it happening at all is worth a search. To find a place where it happens in a healthy and useful way, both for our sakes and for the sake of other people, is a discovery.

So this is one thing the original Christmas story, Emmanuel, God-with-us, points to. It points to and creates community. God is with us, and we are with each other and with God.

Someone did a survey of elderly people in nursing homes. They asked, now that you have time to look back, what are your wishes about the life you've lived? The answers came in this order. First, they said they wished they had loved more people. Second, they wished they had taken more risks. And third, they wished they were sure they had made a difference for good, that they were going to leave some good behind. Love, risk, and making a difference—those are all things that happen when people are part of a good community.

This is something everyone needs. Not everyone finds it. But life without community is dangerous and lonesome. Harry Stack

Sullivan's definition of a sociopath was someone who only had furtive, fleeting involvements with other people. The closer someone is to that, the farther he or she is from community.

Lacking community, people are too easily self-involved: Self-improvement, self-development, and self-awareness take the place of involvement with people and things outside self. Lacking community, people try to replace it with other things: work, wealth, excitement, unusual experiences (either secular or religious). I suspect that both the megachurch and charismatic movements of the last twenty years are examples of that.

If you join this community—really join it, not just formally but personally—your life will change. If you become part of its work and mission, your life will change. If you take its values as seriously as the values that are offered to you everywhere you go, your life will change.

The thing about this Christmas midrash, this application, is that it doesn't end at midnight. There's room for the end of the story to be written for you, and for other people we don't yet know but who will be part of it. It goes on.

Now you know what this congregation is all about. And now you can honestly say you went to church and heard a Christmas sermon that started, and ended, with "Tickle me."

Richard McCandless serves St. Paul's Episcopal Church in Akron, Ohio.

The Messy Magic of Christian Community

Joy Rogers
2 Corinthians 1:23–2:4

There was a street of shops around the corner from our last house. Every fall, the shopkeeper in the corner store put a sign in the window that read:

> *You can help teach your child the values of compassion, responsibility, commitment, respect, friendship and nurturing—all learned so naturally through the magic of pets.*

Every time I passed that sign, it reminded me of what my children have taught me—all through the magic of pets: hysteria, paranoia, frustration, anxiety, and various new techniques for spot removal.

I admit, there has been something of mystery in it all—the purportedly celibate, purportedly male, hamster, who produced a litter of squirming naked hamsterettes—the transfigured rabbit who met his maker due to an unfortunate taste for electrical cords—the ferret with the endearing habit of stealing credit cards from the purses of our dinner guests, usually parishioners.

On the whole, I must agree with the shop window's wisdom. My experience of the magic of pets has been a character-building and character-testing enterprise.

The daily office lectionary for the homiletically adventurous marches us at a rather brisk pace through Paul's Corinthian correspondence at this time of year.

And throughout, the apostle is doing his own kind of advertising; Paul is promoting values and virtues. He is calling his sisters and brothers in Christ to a character-building enterprise—all learned so naturally, through the magic of Christian community.

But there are some ragged edges in this mystical relationship, it would seem. 2 Corinthians 2:4: "For I wrote you out of much distress and anguish of heart and with many tears, not to cause you pain, but to let you know the abundant love that I have for you."

Paul is scarcely a romantic about the possibilities of faith communities. He has known firsthand a fair number of variations on the theme. He writes those famous letters not simply because God's people are once again facing tedious times, but because they are in truth often tedious persons.

He has a lot to say about what his brothers and sisters in Christ have taught him through the magic of Christian community. The list is vaguely familiar—hysteria, paranoia, frustration, anxiety. I don't know about spot removal.

The earliest versions of this enterprise we call Church must have been a tough test for any preacher. It was a pretty feisty household, full of folk who didn't have much else in common except an unreasonable faith that a crucified Jewish carpenter was the Lord of Life.

The heroic and the hysterical, the flawed and the foolish; the guilty, the gullible, and the grieving; the privileged, the pious, and the oppressed. These are the kind of folk that had to figure out how to be the Church—this "company of strangers."

The messy magic of Christian community—scarcely a neat, serene, or efficient way to propagate the faith, if you ask me. The New Testament testifies to the struggles, the outright battles between factions; who is in, and who is out, and how do you tell the difference?

Paul and his letters didn't solve all their problems. But he gives us still some perspective on our own. By his own report, he handles with much nobility of spirit and unswerving courage the apparently easier issues like imperial persecution, the violence of mobs, the accusations and assaults of his former coreligionists.

Time and again, it is the fractiousness, the flaws and fragility of the members of the communities of which he is a part, that reduce him in his communications to something akin to whining. It's his own folk that evoke from the crusty apostle the most anguished, hurting, even defensive responses.

I don't commend that as a model for preaching; but I know something of that struggle in the life of a preacher. So Paul calls me to a new appreciation of his faith communities, and of my own.

However provoked he is by those stupid Galatians, or however aggravating the news from Corinth, it is always clear that Paul knows that he writes to folk who have risked much, indeed risked everything to gather with other unlikely believers: to people who dared to align themselves with each other, despite upbringings and tastes and cultural norms that scorned, even feared such assemblies.

He writes for people who willingly place themselves in new and vulnerable ways under new and uncomfortable rules for relationships. Faith in Jesus Christ is one thing; an enduring relationship with folk with whom you have precious little else in common, and the capacity to make a gentle, faithful, hopeful response to those who treat you with disdain, or worse—that is something else again.

We have heard of martyrdom this week, and most of us must wonder if we could meet that test with faith and courage. But I am reminded by our letter-writing mentor that before Paul was called upon to die for his faith, he had learned a lot about living with the faithful.

Paul wrote letters to his companions in Christ because he had a vision and a passion about what would call forth character worthy of the Christ in people who sought a new kind of personhood. He wrote to them about the necessary virtues for building up communities that would be faithful to God's work and that could live out of the truth of Jesus' Cross.

He wrote a lot of letters, because his congregations weren't very good at Christ-like togetherness.

Twenty centuries later he writes to us, because we still aren't.

Twenty centuries later, we are pushed to struggle with the same feisty, uncomfortable, messy magic that is the Christian community, this transitory one, our local ones, as well as the larger arena:

- extravagantly graced with everything we need to teach us of godly virtue, to fill us with sheer delight in being part of a godly company;
- and annoyingly afflicted with all that can make us crazy—the frustrations, hysteria, fears, anxieties that come from life with other human beings.

And twenty centuries later, we still trust the same truths that our mothers and fathers in faith came to know—that Christian community still beats the world's odds only because it finds enduring meaning and an ongoing mission in the mystery that is the Christ. We preach not ourselves; we proclaim Jesus as Lord and ourselves as servants for Jesus' sake.

Like those fractious Corinthians, preachers and people alike still need to ponder the wisdom that encourages us to persevere and to examine the values and virtues we hold dear in the light of Christ crucified and risen.

We need as well to note the costly nature of our common life. The universe may be friendly, but a faithful preacher of the Gospel will find that the Church is sometimes not. And more crucial, even if the lions are not roaring in the arena, the people who sit in our pews put themselves at risk to be there, in ways we may not ever fully know or understand. They too have placed themselves in vulnerable ways under countercultural and uncomfortable rules for relationships.

In a society whose theme song is "I did it my way," they have dared to align themselves with each other, and with you, with Paul, and his unruly, beloved Corinthians. They have placed themselves in the path of a life-changing, world-shattering Gospel, despite all the forces of our culture that say such choices are foolish, dangerous, or irrelevant.

If we are to preach anyone to faith worth dying for, it means offering them a glimpse of faith that one might live out of. It means preaching not our personal revelation, but from confidence in Christ, and with compassion for his people.

It means staying, not leaving, when the air gets heavy. It means embracing, not excommunicating, when the debates rage about us. For us as for Paul, it may mean tears and anger and arguments, hurt feelings and humbled hopes, when the alternatives are polite niceties or stony silences.

The apostle points me then to the poet:

God does not demand that we give up our personal dignity, that we throw in our lot with random people, that we lose ourselves and turn from all that is not God. God needs nothing, asks nothing, and demands nothing, like the stars. It is a life with God that demands these things....

You do not have to do these things; not at all. God does not, I regret to report, give a hoot. You do not have to do these things—unless you want to know God. They work on you, not on him.

You do not have to sit outside in the dark. If, however, you want to look at the stars, you will find that darkness is necessary. But the stars neither require nor demand it. (Annie Dillard, Teaching a Stone to Talk, p. 31)

I have been known to take issue from time to time with some of the things the apostle says. It is only fair then to put a question or two to the poet. She's good; but she's not quite right—about God not giving a hoot.

If the continuing existence of the Church and her Gospel, preached and proclaimed by the likes of you and me, means anything, it means that God does give a hoot. A big enough hoot to join us in the messy mystery of our very humanity, to join us in the muddled magic of our life together, to hang out with us in mundane materials like bread and wine, to hang for us on a Cross that bears the weight of all our flaws and fragility, our suffering and our guilt.

My sisters and brothers, preach a people to the knowledge of the glory of God in the face of Jesus Christ—the Lord who calls us to follow, and gives us a disconcerting company of fallible, flawed, and sometimes downright irritating siblings to be the only visible, accessible means to a lovely end.

Then, promise your people miraculous birthings, and passionate dyings, and surprising intrusions. Promise them encounters with God, as they collide with one another. For if we cannot recognize Christ in each other, it is hard to know how we will ever meet him at all.

This is our blessing, our call, our mission: the messy, creative, redemptive magic of Christian community. The magic that takes us as we are, and still shows us how we are called to be more; that promises that we will get there only in the company of one another.

Joy Rogers is the Rector of St. Thomas Episcopal Church in Battle Creek, Michigan.

EPILOGUE: Sermon Work as Sacred Gift

It is the final morning of the conference. There have been two sermons preached by every student participant (one prepared before the beginning of the conference, and one presented as an extemporaneous homily—scripture text assigned, less than an hour of preparation time allowed). Each student sermon has been honored by supportive and nurturing, but also by discerning and penetrating, feedback from the other eight students and two staff members who comprise that preacher's small listening group.

There has been formal worship in the morning and the evening of every working conference day. A staff member has preached at each service. Four lectures have been given, and discussions convened. There has been a formal banquet, and a free night on the town. Practically everybody has gotten practically no sleep. Students and staff are simultaneously exhausted and exhilarated.

Students have made an unexpected discovery: "That other seminary" must not be quite so perverse as it is reputed to be—after all, they have laughed and cried, walked and talked, preached and prayed with folks from that seminary. More important, the seminarians have discovered that, in their own generation of people preparing for ordained ministry, there are fifty other folks who care deeply about preaching. A further insight dawns: "Whenever I stand to preach, I know I will never be actually as alone as I may sometimes feel that I am."

All sorts of arrangements have been made, not just to "stay in touch," but to trade sermons—either by tape or by e-mail. And not just finished products, but works in process. Far more important than any theological insight gained, homiletical technique discovered, or even individual friendship formed, however, is the fact that people are heading home (students and staff alike) with a palpable sense of the company of preachers. They no longer have any reason to preach as "Lone Rangers." They realize that, while they may be able to survive as solitary preachers, they are not called to live that way, and they will not be able to thrive that way.

A good lesson for those who, while standing alone in the pulpit or the aisle, may tend to forget that they are never isolated professionals who preach "to" people (let alone "at" them). As preachers, they are sermon conveners. They preach for congregations and with congregations, since, in addition to being an artistic form of rhetorical music, preaching is also (as the title of last year's volume in this series says) "a sacred conversation."

The "conversation" metaphor is a helpful corrective to that of preaching as "rhetorical music." As music, preaching is not a performing art reserved for virtuosi who win and maintain their positions by competition and comparative rating. ("Our preacher is five times better than your preacher—and we pay him the salary to prove it!") No, preaching is a folk art—which does not mean that it is sloppy, undisciplined, just thrown together, or insignificant (theologically or artistically). The point is, rather, that preaching is "of God's people, by God's people, and for God's people." The pulpit is no place for prima donnas.

The work of preaching, then, while an art, is at root a gift. A gift from preacher to people. A gift from people to preacher. A gift of ancient tradition to the contemporary Church, a gift of today's Church to its forbears and to its future offspring. A gift of the Christian community to the world and to God. A gift from God to the preacher, to the community of faith, and to the wider world whom God deeply loves.

That all sounds just lovely when you read it or write it. It sounds positively terrifying when your date with the pulpit is rushing toward you at warp speed. You have done all your homework; you have said all your prayers—and you haven't a clue what you are going to say. It wouldn't be so bad if preaching were all a matter of human achievement. Then you could do more homework, or hire a professional consultant, or any one of a dozen things that could make you more proficient. And, of course, there may be nothing wrong (and sometimes something quite right) in doing such things.

But if the bottom line is that preaching is a *gift*, then, at some point (more probably, at several points), we will find ourselves unable to make any music. And then, although it is against every screaming impulse in our bodies, the only thing we can fruitfully do is to listen as intently and as quietly as we can for the sound of Gospel music.

We may not receive a direct, unequivocal, "Now hear this: Go play that!" (Although, in fact, we might.) Where we may well hear the music is in the songs that still reverberate in the center of our souls—songs previously sung by our preaching sisters and brothers. (There is good theological precedent for this, actually. All sorts of preachers who show up in the texts of scripture can be found, upon close examination, to be singing the songs of their older sisters and brothers.)

But back to the Preaching Excellence Conference. It is the last morning. Breakfast is over. Bags are packed. Rooms are cleared. The bus for the airport is on its way to pick up the troops. It is all over (as they say) but the shouting.

"They," of course, are wrong, as usual. It is all over but the final celebration of Eucharist. "The bread of heaven, broken for you.... Go in peace.... Break the bread of life for the people of God.... Break the bread of life for the life of the world....

But we are getting ahead of ourselves, aren't we? The Sacrament of the Word goes forth before the Sacrament of the Table. And the Sacrament of the Word requires a preacher. A preacher, in this case, who has struggled mightily to shape a timely word that she and her community will he able to sing. How can she be heard, when so many splendid songs have been sung this week already?

They aren't working.

None of the artistic techniques for musical preaching is working.

You have to have raw materials if you're going to be an artist.

You have to hear a melody if you are going to:

discern the pattern of sacred presence;
make connections with raw human reality;
tune the senses of all to the mutual singing;
shape a sermon that resonates with the music.

What if this sermon doesn't work?

Why does preaching have to be a gift?

If sermon work is a sacred gift—well—how come it is so much work? And why do we often have so little to show for it?

Too late. The last words of Matthew 6:24 are proclaimed.

"Praise to you, Lord Christ," say the company of preachers in chorus.

They take their seats. All eyes focus on the lone female figure who stands before them.

No. She isn't "alone." All sorts of sisters and brothers are with her; and the songs of their recent sermons are starting to sing within her.

The struggle ceases.

Here comes the gift.

What can the preacher do, but share what comes?

The Struggle Is the Sermon

Ann Holmes Redding
Psalm 8; Ecclesiastes 3:1, 9–13; 1 Peter 2:11–17; Matthew 6: 19–24

"Imagine the preacher in preparation mode, raw materials spread before her: scripture, soul, mind, newspaper, knowledge of people, needs of the world, tomorrow's liturgy.

"How does it all come together? Is there a nudge, a prodding—a dream, a memory, an insight, an idea, a passion? Maybe even a winged echo?"

Frankly, no. At least, not this time.

This one was a struggle. In a moment of desperation I began to hope for some natural disaster, inconsequential enough to cause no real inconvenience, other than the early end of this conference.

I don't mind decreasing…as long as it's voluntary. I'd like to choose the occasion, not to have my decreasing come in the form of every preacher's nightmare: standing in the pulpit without a word to say.

Such an incident happened in this very pulpit, during one of my many years here on the Seminary Close. The preacher, then a tutor, got up and said that he had nothing to say. Nearly everyone present identified to some degree with his anguish and shame, but I remember most vividly the response of one of my closest friends. She came to me, practically speechless herself. "All I could think of," she said, "was Jesus saying, 'If your son asks you for bread, would you give him a stone?' That's what we got tonight, a stone. We needed bread."

I thought of that tutor as I struggled with this message. And in the midst of my wrestling, a light went on: The struggle itself is the sermon.

The particular intention of this Eucharist is to hold up vocation in daily work. I am struck with the reality that this very conference holds up a particular vocation in *our* daily lives. None of us would be here if preaching were not a vital part of our daily work. We are called to struggle with the Gospel on a daily basis…struggle with it, until like Jacob, we are blessed. Maybe wounded in the process, but blessed. And in turn we share those blessings with God's gathered people.

Today's Gospel is about blessings; treasure, actually. Jesus speaks of treasure in a rather puzzling way. "Do not store up for yourselves treasures on earth, where moth and rust consume and where thieves come in and steal. Store up for yourselves treasures in *heaven*…. For where your treasure is, there will your heart be also." It's not, "Where your heart is, there will your treasure be," but the other way around. He's not saying, "Follow your heart and the treasures from heaven will follow." Instead Jesus is saying, "Amass treasures in heaven, and your heart will follow." How does one amass treasures in heaven in the first place? The clue comes at the end of the passage: "No one is able to slave for two masters.... You are not able to slave for God and mammon."

※

We store up treasures in heaven by serving God, by answering God's call on our lives. If we do so, Jesus promises that our heart will follow.

Years ago, I had a close encounter of the vocational kind with the religious life. I got as far as an interview with the Mother Superior. This wise woman had been speaking with aspirants for quite a long time and knew much about what vocation was, and what vocation wasn't. Mother Boniface said that, even if your vocation seems to come out of the blue, you can recognize it, because it makes the many various fragments of your life come together in a pattern and make sense. Your heart recognizes the pattern as coming home.

This week I have seen many signs, not only of calling, but of the heart's recognition of and response to calling. I've seen it in attentiveness and care about the task of preaching. I've seen it in the respect given to others who care about preaching.

I have also seen another kind of convergence of treasure and heart, of God's purpose and our desires and needs. Some of us recognize that it is by God's *mercy* we are preachers. We *need* to be preachers. Anne Bartlett put it this way: "Maybe when I grow up, I won't have to be a preacher. But now, it is what saves me."

I know what she means. I know, for example, that I am the kind of person who absolutely needs to be in church at least every Sunday. So God has given me the grace of a calling that necessitates I be in church and even pays me (not a lot, granted) to be there.

I need to be a preacher. I need to do the work required of a preacher. I need to do the reading and the struggling; I need to do the praying and the mulling. I need to do the proclaiming. I need to do all of this work; but I am the kind of person who probably wouldn't choose to do it on my own initiative. I wouldn't think of doing it if I did not, by the mercy of God, have this calling.

So, according to divine economy, we are called to this task that we need to do for our own soul's sake, and we are given a passion to do it. We are called to a task we love to do and we need to do and one in which, amazingly enough, God uses us.

One Sunday I was called to the phone about an hour after church to take an urgent call from a parishioner. When I got to the phone, I realized that both the woman and her husband were on the line. I asked, "What's wrong?" The wife answered, "Nothing's really wrong. We were just arguing about your sermon and wanted to ask you some questions. Now did you mean...?" Then she and her husband launched into a discussion of my sermon, while I sat on the other end of the phone, amazed. I realized that my sermon hadn't really started with me. It had been started in me. And it certainly wasn't finished, because Karen and Al were still preaching it. At these moments I don't really feel pride in myself. Instead I have humility thrust upon me; I am overawed and deeply grateful that God might choose to use me as I do a task I need to do for my own good.

It is no accident that the moments like this one, where I have the most profound sense of the treasure of my calling, are the moments when I realize most deeply how God uses it for the people of God. Our hearts move to where our treasure is because God is connecting us to others for the purpose of building the kingdom.

My father, who as the first and for years the only black lawyer in the state of Delaware, was a civil rights pioneer. When he heard I was seminary bound, he said to me, "But, baby, you're not going to be a *preacher*, are you? If you want to help people, be a lawyer." To allay his fears, I said to him that I was going to be a priest, but that I would preach from time to time. Today, I am willing to be called and to be a preacher. I am willing to take on the lifelong struggle with the glory of the word. I am glad that I am in such good company.

I am never good at saying good-bye, so I struggled particularly with the end of this sermon. Then I realized that I had a wish list for you, and I will end with that.

I wish you the will to decrease and the desire to get out of the way.

I wish you sanctuaries filled with the sweet fragrance of Christians.

I wish you the willingness to embrace the many messy minor martyrdoms of daily living.

I wish you the big-heartedness and humor to deal with tedious companions and troublesome traveling partners.

I wish you a home in the pulpit.

I wish you the company of angels, Eastern and Western, to surround your proclamation.

I wish you the strength to struggle with the story and the patience to tell it again and again and again.

Ann Holmes Redding teaches at the Interdenominational Theological Center in Atlanta, Georgia.

The Preaching Excellence Program—1997

(This abbreviated conference schedule from the 1997 Preaching Excellence Program puts much of this book's material in context.)

The General Theological Seminary
New York, NY
May 31-June 6, 1997

CONFERENCE AGENDA & SCHEDULE

Saturday, May 31, 1997

5:00 p.m.	Evensong & Sermon: *The Rev. William Hethcock, preaching*
7:30 p.m.	Conference Orientation—Seabury Auditorium

Monday, June 2nd

8:00 a.m.	Holy Eucharist & Sermon: *The Rev. Joseph Burnett, preaching*
9:00 a.m.-Noon	Preaching Groups
2:30-4:30 p.m.	Lecture: "Distinctive Aspects of Anglican Preaching" *The Rev. Dr. Mitties De Champlain*
5:00 p.m.	Evening Prayer & Sermon: *The Rev. Anne K. Bartlett, preaching*

Tuesday, June 3rd

8:00 a.m.	Holy Eucharist & Sermon: *The Rev. Dr. Linda Clader, preaching*
9:00 a.m.-12:00	Preaching Groups
12:15-12:45 p.m.	Lunch Presentation: The Episcopal Evangelism Foundation and Its Ministries *Roger Alling & Dr. A. Gary Shilling*
2:00 p.m.-4:00 p.m.	Lecture: "Stick It in Your Ear: Preaching to be Heard" *The Rev. Dr. Neil Alexander*
5:00 p.m.	Evening Prayer & Sermon: *The Rev. Michael Goldberg, preaching*
7:30 p.m.	A Roundtable on Sermons and Their Preparation: Conference Staff

Conference Schedule

Wednesday, June 4th

8:00 a.m.	Holy Eucharist & Sermon: *The Rev. Roger Alling, preaching*
9:00 a.m.-Noon	Conference Lectures : The Rev. Dr. Thomas G. Long, Frances Landey Patton Professor of Preaching & Worship, Princeton Theological Seminary
2:00-4:00 p.m.	Lecture: "Preaching the Good: Homiletics from a Moral Theological Perspective" *The Rev. Thomas E. Breidenthal, D. Phil: Associate Professor of Moral Theology in the John Henry Hobart Chair of Christian Ethics, General Theological Seminary.*
5:00 p.m.	Evening Prayer & Sermon: *The Rev. Joy Rogers, preaching*

Thursday, June 6th

8:00 a.m.	Morning Prayer & Sermon: *The Rev. Jane Sigloh, preaching*
9:00 a.m.-12:00	Preaching Groups
12:10	Holy Eucharist & Sermon: *The Rev. Dr. Neil Alexander, preaching*

2:00 p.m.	Preaching Groups
	    Extemporaneous
	    Homilies

5:00 p.m.	Evening Prayer & Sermon: *The Rev. Dr. Charles Rice, preaching*

Friday, June 6th

8:00 a.m.	Holy Eucharist & Sermon: *The Rev. Ann Redding, preaching*

Staff Members:
1997 Preaching Excellence Program

Rev. Neil Alexander
The School of Theology
The University of the South
Sewanee, Tenn.

Rev. Roger Alling
The Episcopal Evangelism
  Foundation, Inc.
Camp Hill, Pa.

Rev. Anne Bartlett
Parish of St. John the Baptist
Portland, Oreg.

Rev. Linda Clader
The Church Divinity School
  of the Pacific
Berkeley, Calif.

Rev. Mitties McDonald De Champlain
The Fuller Theological Seminary
Pasadena, Calif.

Rev. William Hethcock
The School of Theology
The University of the South
Sewanee, Tenn.

Rev. Joy Rogers
St. Thomas Episcopal Church
Battle Creek, Mich

Rev. Joe Burnett
Trinity Episcopal Church
Hattiesburg, Miss.

Rev. Michael Goldberg
St. Augustine's Church
Vero Beach, Florida

Rev. Ann Redding
Interdenominational
  Theological Center
Atlanta, Ga.

Rev. Charles Rice
Drew University Seminary
Madison, N. J.

Rev. Jane Sigloh
Emmanuel Church
Staunton, Va.

Rev. Thomas G. Long
Director of Congregational
  Resources
Presbyterian Publishing Corporation
Louisville, KY 40202-1396

Rev. Thomas Breidenthal
Associate Professor of Moral
  Theology
The General Theological Seminary
New York, N. Y.

Winners in the 1997 Best Sermon Competition

Rev. Sara Scott Wingo
St. Philip's Church
Fort Payne, Birmingham, Ala.

Rev. James Adams
St. Thomas Episcopal Church
Hanover, N. H.

Rev. Penelope Duckworth
Stanford Canterbury Foundation
Stanford, Calif.

Reverenda Sylvia Vasquez
St. Paul's Episcopal Church
San Antonio, Tex.

Rev. Lisa Cressman
Trinity Episcopal Church
Indianapolis, Ind.

Rev. Richard McCandless
St. Paul's Episcopal Church
Akron, Ohio

Rev. Stephen Weissman
Pike County Episcopal Churches
Louisiana, Mo.

Rev. Karen Johnson
Christ Episcopal Church
Rockville, Md.

Rev. John Conrad
St. Mark's Episcopal Church
Glendale, Calif.

Rev. Leander Harding
St. John's Episcopal Church
Stamford, Conn.